Annemarie Cross has written a cracker of a [barcode: I0069322]
Thought Leader".

As a proponent of Authority Marketing I a
at business conferences on the value of content and sharing how
podcasting is one of the most sought-after content mediums you
can create.

"Industry Thought Leader" covers this concept in exceptional
detail. I love how Annemarie has exposed some of the common
misconceptions around podcasting and laid out a clear step by
step guide to not only getting started in podcasting, but how to
manage the mindset challenges that are very real in the journey
that is ahead to becoming highly influential.

As one of Australia's leading podcasters and influencers Annemarie
walks the talk that is laid out in this must read book.

Adam Houlahan
www.adamhoulahan.com

International Keynote Speaker
Amazon Best-Selling Author

In an increasingly noisy world, your personal brand and unique
thought leadership is an extremely effective way to reach people
with your message, and create a sustainable business.

Podcasting can be a brilliant platform for sharing your message,
and in *Industry Thought Leaders,* Annemarie helps you identify how
to do this effectively.

I not only follow Annemarie's work, but I've also interviewed her on my podcast, and she absolutely walks her talk.

She's a leading authority in helping entrepreneurs use the vehicle of podcasting to position their authority, and this book clearly shows you the exact steps you need to take your podcast to build influence AND create profits with your podcast.

Samantha Riley,
SamanthaRiley.Global

Creator of the Thought Leaders Business Lab Podcast

In a world of so-called leaders touting authenticity there are very few people who actually speak, act and educate from a place of true heart centred motivation.

Annemarie is that person.

Annemarie has created a podcasting platform that launches dreams, visions and positive change.

I applaud her.

As an international speaker and edu-tainer I am constantly coming across unfulfilled genius. Participating in Annemarie's Ambitious Entrepreneur Show was a pleasure and filled my heart knowing that unfulfilled genius' are being brought forward to shine their light.

Justin Cunningham
International Speaker/Edu-tainer & Business Resultant
www.justincunninghamonline.com

INDUSTRY
THOUGHT
LEADER

How to Go from Invisible to Influential (and Profitable) with a Podcast

ANNEMARIE CROSS

Industry Thought Leader
How to Go From Invisible to Influential (and Profitable) with a Podcast
© 2019 Annemarie Cross

Communicate Now Pty Ltd
PO Box 91, Hallam Victoria 3803
Australia

ISBN 978-0-6485020-0-5 paperback
ISBN 978-0-6485020-1-2 eBook

This is dedicated to all of my wonderful clients (past, current and future) – thank you for allowing me to be part of your podcast publishing journey.

Here's to impacting in the world – with YOUR message!

CONTENTS

FOREWORD

Going back 8 years now, I first met Annemarie when she was doing one of our Video Marketing Courses. It was one of Australia's first Video Marketing courses and it showed back then that Annemarie was going the be one to embrace new technology and make it work.

It wasn't long after that when I saw her embrace the new platform called Podcasting. Back when it was new. Back when all the gadgets and apps weren't around to systemize everything and back when it was just damn hard work.

Starting with 'Career Success Radio' her first podcast (which launched in 2008) Annemarie has certainly had some ups and downs in this arena but has always come through, not only making it work but sharing what didn't helping others to avoid the early mistakes.

It wasn't long before she was given the Title as 'The Podcasting Queen'. A title I completely agree with.

This book is a down to earth look at the real ups and downs, benefits and pitfalls of Podcasting. It pulls back the curtain and exposes the false glamour side that some portray yet shows the enormous positioning benefits when implemented correctly. As an Authority Marketing Coach and Mentor it felt hypocritical not using a Podcast as a medium to complement my other communication channels.

There was only one person to turn to and Annemarie gave me some excellent advice that helped me avoid a lot of heartache.

You will get extreme value in just the Myth Busting Section. Many people start a podcast thinking it to be a cash cow or event a ticket to instant stardom. Annemarie's no bull approach to writing it like it is will set you straight.

The rest of the book is a roadmap for your success. Follow it through with pen in hand and take notes. And then more importantly IMPLEMENT them.

In just the first few months of having my Podcast and implementing Annemarie's strategies it has opened doors and I have met people that I would never have been able to meet.

Enjoy the rest of the book and I look forward to hearing you shortly on the airwaves.

Steve Brossman
The Authority Catalyst
www.SteveBrossman.com

ACKNOWLEDGEMENTS

First and foremost, I want to give a shout-out to my former co-host – Keith Keller, because were it not for our conversations all those years ago where we said, "Let's start a podcast!", none of these would have been possible.

The difference, of course, with our very first podcast (which was more like an online radio show) was that everything was live-to-air, meaning there were many challenges we had to overcome. Like the times where one of us was kicked off the switchboard; the time where our guests didn't show up on time because they miscalculated the time zones, and we had to fill an entire hour of the show on our own; or that time where it took us months to arrange special guest, Ivan Misner (from BNI International), then six minutes into the show, we were both kicked off the switchboard, leaving our concerned guest to fend for himself while we both desperately tried to dial back in.

Those first two years were fun AND challenging, however, a wonderful training ground. Thank you for your friendship, Keith.

To my husband, Garry, thank you for your unconditional support all of these years amidst the highs and lows that entrepreneurship brings. As an avid learner and someone who gets restless when working on similar projects for a period of time, this meant I was off attending courses, trainings, certifications and conferences around the globe.

What's interesting is that that crazy little idea I had over 10 years ago to start a podcast stuck! Who knew it would turn into a full-time business all of these years later, being a culmination of everything I've learned over the last two decades in business.

Thank you for believing in me, even when (I'm sure you thought) I was off chasing another one of my 'crazy ideas'.

I love you.

INTRODUCTION

The fact that you're reading this book tells me three things:

- You have a desire to take your influence, impact and income to a MUCH greater level.
- You have a body of knowledge and experience that has been developed over a number of years and you've supported clients in making transformational changes in their lives and/or businesses.
- You want to find out how you can leverage a podcast to make a real difference while simultaneously building your visibility, credibility and authority to become known as a Thought Leader in your industry.

If that sounds like you and you resonate with either one (or ALL) of the following statements, you are in the right place:

- You want to make a REAL difference in the world.
- You want to share your message in a bigger way.
- You're a Change Maker (even though you may not necessarily refer to yourself this way); you are ambitious and feel compelled to get your message out to make a bigger impact.
- You want the freedom to be able to make your own decisions and follow your own dreams (rather than someone else's).
- You want to create an income that supports your dreams, your family and your lifestyle.
- You have a deep desire to challenge the status quo in your industry because you're tired of the BS.

- You want to be recognised as a Thought Leader in your industry – even though, if you're honest, there are moments when you doubt you have what it takes and will find yourself asking: 'Who do I think I am to become known as a Thought Leader?'

If any of these sounds like you – welcome friend! You are in the right place!

My Journey into the World of Podcasting

I started my first podcast in 2008. At the time, I was working in the career industry as a Personal Brand Strategist and Career Coach/Consultant in my own business. As well as working with my own private clients, I had secured a contract with a major career organization in the USA, which entailed interview coaching and writing resumes.

In 2008, the global economy crashed, resulting in tens of thousands of people worldwide becoming unemployed. There were accountants and senior executives, anxious to find work, who were applying for bookkeeping and other administrative-type roles that were paying only $8/hour. A rate that was low, even for bookkeepers and administrative staff, let alone senior executives. It was desperate times. People were doing what they could to survive.

However, it was the doom and gloom portrayed by the media that annoyed me the most. And, it was this constant portrayal of negativity that prompted a colleague and me to start our podcast - Career Success Radio.

We knew while things were difficult, there was always hope. People needed to change their approach (and attitude) to their job search. However, we understood that it would be difficult for them to find any sliver of hope if they continued to listen to the doom and gloom. So, each week we shared our inspirational message and career insights on how to find a job despite the market downturn.

In the two years we produced our podcast, we achieved results that exceeded our expectations. Accomplishments we are both still extremely proud of, include:

- Being listened to in over 100 countries.
- Gaining more exposure than any other marketing strategy we had implemented in our business.
- Being seen as Thought Leaders in our industry and pioneers in the podcasting space, as we were among just a handful of career-focused podcasts at that time.
- Building friendships with guests from around the globe – many of whom we would never have met were it not for our podcast.

Despite these wins, there was one area we continued to struggle in, and one of the main reasons we stopped production. We struggled to monetize our podcast, so we parted ways.

Hindsight is a wonderful teacher. Looking back, there were definitely gaps in our strategy. We even sought advice from a few mentors who suggested we offer sponsorships. However, being that podcasting was relatively new at that time (and we often had to explain what a podcast was and how people could access our show) our small, yet devoted audience wasn't a consideration for sponsors who were still heavily investing in radio, television and print advertising.

Now, of course, we recognise that a business leveraging a podcast as part of their marketing can generate incredible influence, impact and income with a small, niched devoted audience – if they have the right strategy in place. Back then, we didn't.

Who is this Book For (and NOT For)

If you've heard that podcasting is a great way to get your message out – it is. However, if you're looking for a quick and easy way to get your podcast up and running – this book is not for you. There are plenty of free resources online to help you.

However, if you're interested in building your reputation as an Industry Thought Leader, while generating leads, enquiries, paying clients, and other opportunities with your podcast and you're willing to take the necessary steps, time, and dedication to focus on what's important when it comes to your message and the content you produce, then this book is for you.

What to Expect from this Book

When people typically think of podcasting their immediate thought is: "What technology should I use to record my podcast?" As a Change Maker and aspiring Thought Leader there are more important things you need to clarify first, before you concern yourself with technology.

Part 1: Busting Common Podcasting Myths

With the rise of popularity in the podcasting space there's a lot of MIS-information that is irrelevant, untrue, and/or misleading.

Especially when it comes to Change Makers and aspiring Thought Leaders and how they can leverage a podcast to help build their influence, impact and income.

We'll start off by debunking some of the common myths; information that is out-dated and untrue about podcasting that as a Change Maker and aspiring Thought Leader you need to know.

Part 2: How to Monetize your Podcast as a Thought Leader

While there are multiple ways to generate income from a podcast as a professional service-based business you are selling your knowledge, skills and experience - your Intellectual Property.

I'll show you five ways you can monetize your message and your expertise through a podcast.

Part 3: How to Define and Position Your Thought Leadership Message with a Podcast: The Steps

Here's where we'll dive into each of the steps you'll need to follow to create a message that cuts through the noise, while engaging, educating, and enticing your ideal client to want to know more, so you can begin to generate influence, impact and income from your very first episode.

You'll be introduced to the following models:

- The Podcast Profit Framework
- The Podcast Profit Formula
- The Podcast Profit Pipeline

The Framework, the Formula, and the Funnel (i.e. Pipeline).

Part 4: Winning Mindset of a Thought Leader

While you can have the right strategy, tactic and systems in place, you can still struggle to create a podcast that generates the influence, impact and income you desire if you don't have the right mindset. This part of the book will help you break through common barriers that can prevent you from stepping out and sharing your message in a much bigger way.

Part 5: Tools and Technology

Now that you have the right strategy, tactic, and streamlined system in place as well as the winning mindset of a Thought Leader, we'll cover the tools and technologies you'll need to produce, publish, and promote your podcast. I'll share some low-cost and no-cost tools to get you started, including what we're using to produce our podcasts.

One last thought...

Before we dive in, you may have a similar question to one I'm often asked: "How did you become known as 'The Podcasting Queen?'" That's a great question. In fact, someone once congratulated me on how I had branded myself 'The Podcasting Queen.'

"While I'd like to take the credit - I can't," I explained. "In fact, it was only after years of guests and colleagues referring to me as the queen of podcasting that I finally decided to 'get over myself' and embrace the title, as for years, I felt uncomfortable when people would refer to me this way."

When I shared this with her, she asked whether I had any tips on how to get people to call you the 'queen' of anything.

It was an interesting question: How do you become recognised in a specific area (i.e. that influential voice) so that your community begins to refer to you this way and recognises you as an Industry Thought Leader? Perhaps even before you do so yourself?

When I looked back over my career, I had been doing numerous podcast interviews and connecting with guests from all over the world for years. Interviewing others was something I loved to do, so it was something I did, week after week, year after year. In fact, had you told me over a decade ago that podcasting would become my full-time business, I wouldn't have believed you.

So, based on my own experience my response to her was:

"Love what you do and get good at it - REALLY good at it. And, if it aligns with your strengths - it'll show, often to others first."

My friend, that's my advice to you too as you seek to build your reputation as an Industry Thought Leader. Get totally clear on what you love to do and ensure it aligns with your innate strengths. Then get good at it. REALLY good at it, by doing it day in and day out. Then capture that message and passion in your podcast so you can take your message to the world and impact others through the ongoing value you provide. People will notice. And, soon they'll be referring to you as that go-to person. An Industry Thought Leader.

Are you ready?

Let's begin…

PART 1

BUSTING COMMON PODCASTING MYTHS

SIX COMMON PODCASTING MYTHS

Before we dive into the 'How Tos' of building your Thought Leadership message and sharing it with the world through your own podcast, let's address some common podcasting myths. That way you can eliminate misleading information and begin to focus on the RIGHT things with your Thought Leader Podcast.

Myth 1: Anyone can start a podcast: Just press record and you're set.

Anyone can. But it doesn't mean they should.

I'll often say:

"Just because you CAN record a podcast - doesn't mean you should. Because without planning, strategy, and a clear PURPOSE in your message, it's just NOISE. And, sadly, you could tarnish your reputation and limit your ability to build your Thought Leadership, and ultimately your influence, impact and income."

Myth 2: You need a list to successfully launch your podcast. Build your list first.

Think you need a list first before you launch your podcast? You don't. In fact, do the opposite. Implement the Thought Leader Podcast Series tactic and use that to build your list of ideal clients and nurture your new connections into leads and ultimately paying customers from your very first episode.

You can start with a list of 0, and begin to monetize your podcast from your very first episode with a Thought Leader Podcast Series.

Myth 3: Get the right microphone and you're set.

You can't edit and mix irrelevant information into compelling content that empowers your audience and entices them to want to know more about you and how you can support them, even if you have the most expensive microphone. You just can't.

Focus on defining your clear, cut-through Thought Leadership Message BEFORE you concern yourself with the make or model of microphone. #MessageBEFOREMicrophone

Myth 4: You need to achieve new & noteworthy status to make an impact.

Stop focusing on vanity numbers. It's a distraction. I'd rather have a small number of listeners who are highly engaged with my content, who are connecting with me, sharing my content, and investing in my services than millions of downloads with no impact on their lives or on the growth of my business.

Myth 5: Monetize your podcast through sponsorships/ advertising and/or listener support.

As an aspiring Thought Leader your Thought Leadership message, which leads to your paid programs and offerings, is the best way to monetize your podcast. Focus on THAT first and foremost. Not selling someone else's products or services.

Myth 6: You need an ongoing podcast to build thought leadership and paying clients.

No you don't. Create a 3-Part Thought Leader Podcast Series and leverage that to continue building brand awareness, your list, your leads, and ultimately paying clients. Then, if you decide to have an ongoing podcast, you've now got a list of existing listeners who you can leverage and garner support from as you launch your ongoing podcast.

Now that we have busted some of the common podcasting myths, let's look at what you can do to increase your impact, influence and income with a podcast. We'll start with monetization strategies.

PART 2

HOW TO MONETIZE YOUR PODCAST AS A THOUGHT LEADER

CHAPTER 1

START WITH THE END IN MIND

When planning a holiday, you'd hardly jump in the car, or get on a plane with the intention of spending your holiday wherever you end up. Instead, you (a) decide where you want to go and then (b) plan how you're going to get there in the best possible way.

When I was in the career industry working with Senior Executives and Professionals, I would often see people spend more time planning their annual vacations than they did planning their career goals. Sadly, this happens with business owners, too. They don't set clear goals, nor do they take the right action steps to support them in achieving their goals. These business owners end up giving up when they fail to generate results.

This also happens to businesses that want to start a podcast without having a clear goal in mind, the right strategy, and relevant action steps. So they either give up after they fail to generate the results they had hoped for, or they never get around to launching their podcast.

I'm determined not to let this happen to you with your podcast. So, in the next chapter let's identify which monetization strategies best align with you and your goals. Doing this IS 'starting with the end in mind'.

CHAPTER 2

FIVE WAYS TO MONETIZE YOUR THOUGHT LEADERSHIP MESSAGE WITH A PODCAST

Many business owners I've spoken to believe they're going to monetize their podcast by increasing their reach and audience numbers so they can attract sponsors for their show. Generating income from sponsors (i.e. advertisers) where you are promoting another company's product and services is certainly an option, and something I have also done previously.

However, as a Change Maker and aspiring Thought Leader, I encourage you to focus on monetizing your own products and services, rather than someone else's. Therefore External and Internal Sponsorships is something I'll cover last.

Be mindful that some monetization strategies will generate income fairly soon, while others may take some time to build the necessary momentum required to bring in a steady flow of leads, enquiries and ultimately paying customers. If you're willing to put in the work required to generate the best results, and are patient and committed to remaining focused and consistent as you take the right action steps to build momentum, your hard work will pay off.

Remember, every opportunity that enables you to get in front of your ideal client where you can provide value, while showcasing your expertise and continuing to build 'know, like and trust,' is invaluable. This is what you should be focusing on, continuously. And, your podcast can and will play an integral role in this process when you have the right strategy in place.

Let's review some of the ways I've been able to monetize my podcasts, which you can consider as part of your monetization strategy.

1) Build Brand Awareness & Authority

Monetization Method 1: Build brand awareness and credibility as an authority in your industry.

Every time someone listens to your podcast, whether you are interviewing a guest or you're sharing insights yourself, will impact your reputation. A large majority of my podcasts involve me interviewing guests. However, while my guests are sharing their expertise, I continue to validate their responses with my experience and understanding, while weaving in titbits, insights and stories throughout the interview, which adds more value to the conversation.

Note: I never overpower the conversation, but rather add value and depth where and when appropriate.

Remember, podcast listeners who come back regularly, do so because of you. While the content must always be relevant and valuable they return for each of your shows because they are interested in learning more from you, which provides you with another opportunity to continue building a relationship and that all important 'know, like and trust'.

11

They can learn this content from dozens – even hundreds of other podcasts, but they choose to subscribe and listen to your podcast, because of you. They appreciate your unique approach, your attitude as well as the experience you create on your podcast. They value the insights and expertise you bring to the conversation, even if you are interviewing guests.

After launching just three episodes of Women in Leadership Podcast, two business owners searched for the term: 'brand and business consultant.' They found my website, listened to the three podcasts, rang me, and enrolled into one of my VIP programs. They hadn't heard of me before that time, and they hadn't listened to any of my other podcasts either.

However, those three episodes (where I was interviewing guests), along with the content they viewed on my website all contributed to validating my expertise. They knew they wanted to work with me and rang me with a few further questions – one of which was: "How can I work with you? Which of your programs do you recommend?"

I secured a speaking opportunity for a local Economic Business Development Department for a local council, who found my website, listened to a number of my podcasts, and confirmed that my expertise and the value I could offer their members, was exactly what they were looking for.

These are just a few examples of the opportunities my podcasts have generated for me, and they can happen for you too. Your listener could be a future VIP client or an event co-ordinator who is looking for a speaker for their next event, or a joint venture partner looking for someone with your expertise to add to their referral list.

Therefore, it's important to be intentional and strategic as you create your digital footprint and continue to build brand awareness and credibility as an authority in your industry.

2) Build Your List with Your Ideal Client

Monetization Method 2: Build your list and begin to nurture your list into leads, enquiries, and ultimately into paying customers.

This method is by far my favourite because when set up correctly can continue to work for you 24/7, 365 days a year. You guide people to your free lead generation opt-in (i.e. your Irresistible Signature Giveaway, as I call it) and then through your email nurturing sequence, which encourages a purchase or a phone call - particularly if you're screening prospective clients for your high-level coaching program. Therefore, it's important to continue growing your list by offering a free resource (i.e. free lead generation opt-in) that requires someone to provide their name and email address (at a minimum) in exchange for access to the free resource.

You may have heard that email is dead and that no one reads emails anymore? This couldn't be farther from the truth. I'll often get emails from subscribers, telling me how much they enjoy reading my newsletters. They continue to appreciate the inspirational and informative content I provide.

'Email is dead' may be their truth because prospective customers aren't engaging with their emails, because they haven't clearly defined their message, or they failed to provide content that was of value. It may take some time for your new subscriber to become a client. However, guess who they're going to reach out to once they're ready to make a decision. You! Because you've continued to position yourself as a Thought Leader in your industry and you've remained top of mind through your newsletters.

I've had people reach out to me 18 months after they initially accessed my Irresistible Signature Giveaway. They weren't ready yet back then; however, they were now, and I was the only person they would consider working with. The Irresistible Signature Giveaway I recommend you create (and is what I'm helping all of my VIP clients create) is their Thought Leader Podcast Series.

We'll dive deeper into that topic later in the book, Part 3: The Steps, Chapter 4: Tactic.

3) Build Relationships with Guests

Monetization Method 3: Develop Joint Venture, Referral Partners and other opportunities from podcast guests.

As an Extroverted Introvert, going to networking events and conferences where I don't know many people pushes me right out of my comfort zone.

While I do attend selected networking events and conferences, being able to leverage my podcast to build relationships with people, which develops into Joint Venture collaborations, referral relationships and other opportunities (such as speaking and being interviewed on their podcasts) has worked well for me.

First and foremost, I'm always looking for guests who can add real value to my audience. That's a given. However, I'm also looking for people who are working with my ideal client and who are offering a product and/or service that is complimentary to what I'm offering.

This has led to many opportunities, including:

- Invitations to speak on Online Summits and Telesummits (alongside other 6- and 7-figure Brand and Business Thought Leaders);
- Invitations to speak at in-person events;
- Joint Venture opportunities;
- Invitation to be a guest on their podcast;
- Referral opportunities, to name a few.

The list of opportunities is vast. You just need to identify which opportunities you can leverage and set about finding people who you would like to work with and reach out to them.

4) Build Direct Business with Guests

Monetization Method 4: Generate enquiries and business from podcast guests.

While this option has never been an intentional one for me, it has happened on a number of occasions, and continues to do so.

Please note, I never set out to compel a guest to work with me. However, as I've mentioned previously, when you are clear on your expertise, it's unique and you're seen as a Thought Leader in your industry, you deliver exceptional value, and you create an incredible environment where your guest feels valued (because they are), then business happens.

Every interaction speaks your brand. And, your interaction with your guest may just pique their interest to want to know more about the work you do. I've had guests invest in my Private VIP

Thought Leader Branding Programs, my Thought Leader Podcast Series offering, and my Podcasting with Purpose Training Course, to name a few.

One guest hired me to do some professional voiceover work for an app. He was adding some educational videos to his app and needed a voiceover professional. After our interview he was so impressed, he asked if I was interested in working with him. The rest is history and my voice now guides his clients to use his app.

As I said, when you get your podcast out there, opportunities just happen. But, ONLY when you have a created a podcast with purpose!

5) Build (External & Internal) Sponsorship Relationships

Monetization Method 5: Sponsorships

As mentioned earlier in this chapter, many business owners believe that monetizing their podcasts will come from sponsorships and advertising. As a Professional Service-based business with expertise to offer, I encourage you to focus on promoting your own products and services, rather than someone else's.

While I have monetized my podcast with external sponsorships in the past, in the last few years I have turned away dozens upon dozens of expressions of interest from businesses interested in sponsoring my podcasts. Instead, I've gone the route of Internal Sponsorships, which is a far better option for Change Makers and aspiring Thought Leaders.

Let's look at External Sponsorships first:

a) External Sponsorships

Be mindful that it can take time to build 'know, like and trust' with your audience, and that relationship can be tarnished quickly if they sense you're trying to make a quick buck from a product and/or service provider. Unless these potential sponsors align with your brand message and you know they provide exceptional products and/or services that would be of value to your audience, you should reconsider allowing them to sponsor your show.

All of the sponsors I've had on the show were either previous guests who aligned with my core values and had information I knew would benefit my audience, or, their product and/or service, was something I'd used myself and therefore knew it would benefit my audience. My sponsorship package involved a 12-week season. For three shows I'd feature a 5-minute 'sponsor spotlight segment' where I interviewed the sponsor about the uses and benefits of their product/service, and how my listeners could benefit from their product/service.

Then in the subsequent 9 weeks, I'd share a 30-second educational tip about that product/service with a call to action directing people back to the sponsor's website. This worked well for a number of seasons; however, it is not something I continue to do as it's not part of my overall short- or long-term strategy.

If you decide to offer External Sponsorships, be mindful that the level of trust you've built with your audience is invaluable, whether you have an audience of 100, 1,000, 10,000 or more. Plus, each podcast episode that showcases your sponsor has the opportunity to be found by their ideal client 24/7, 365 days/year as you continue to promote the show and as people discover the show. Unlike traditional media, which may have a larger audience, it however has a finite life span. Once it's been broadcasted live to air, that's it.

b) Internal Sponsorships

The way we are using sponsors for all our podcasts and as part of our short- and long-term plan is a strategy we recommend to all of our clients, which is Internal Sponsorships. Internal Sponsorships involve our Signature Programs and/or sub-brands, which become named sponsors of our show(s), with the goal of raising awareness of our offerings and/or sub-brands.

For example: My Signature Program: 'Podcasting with Purpose' is used in my intro and outro. When I'm introducing my guest, I say:

"Welcome to another episode of Ambitious Entrepreneur Show, this is episode 265 brought to you by Podcasting with Purpose, helping you become an influential voice in your industry with a podcast. I'm your host – Annemarie Cross, The Podcasting Queen."

The outro is pre-recorded with the same voiceover professional and music as the intro, with the words:

"You've been listening to the Ambitious Entrepreneur Show, brought to you by PodcastingWithPurpose.com – Stand Out, Be Heard - INFLUENCE. Want to influence change with your own podcast? Access our free podcast training including our no-cost and low-cost tools to get you started at www.PodcastingWithPurpose.com/minitraining that's www.PodcastingWithPurpose.com/minitraining."

One of our sub-brands 'BE the Difference Movement' is a Facebook Group where we are building relationships with Change Makers and aspiring Thought Leaders. The outro is pre-recorded with the same voiceover professional and music as the intro, with the words:

"You've been listening to the Ambitious Entrepreneur Show brought to you by Be the Difference Movement.com – Changing the World, One message at a time. Do you feel called to influence real change with your message? Join our supportive group of like-minded influencers, thought leaders and disruptors at www.BetheDifferenceMovement.com that's www.BetheDifferenceMovement.com."

PART 3

HOW TO DEFINE AND POSITION YOUR THOUGHT LEADERSHIP MESSAGE WITH A PODCAST

CHAPTER 1

THE IMPORTANCE OF CONTEXT

Have you ever listened to a podcast and within the first few sentences, or even a few words, you're thinking: "Huh?" "What the?" "Not relevant for me."

Sadly, it happens. A lot. Whether it's a bad choice of music, poorly selected voiceover professional, with the host(s) rambling at the beginning of the show. Or, perhaps a combination of all of these things, leaving you confused, disinterested, and moving on. A lack of 'context' will do that. And, it's one of the quickest ways to lose a listener's attention.

Without context, we're left thinking:

- What am I going to learn?
- What does this have to do with me?
- Why should I invest my valuable time listening to this?

Avoid creating a situation which can cause your listener to become confused and/or assume the podcast has no relevance to them. Give them context. Paint the picture. Set the scene. Create an experience - an experience that resonates with and captures and maintains your ideal client's attention from the beginning of the podcast until the very end.

The following chapters will help you do just that starting with what you should focus on first.

INTRODUCING THE PODCAST PROFIT FORMULA

In Busting Common Podcasting Myths, I recommended not focusing on technology first. This chapter dives a little deeper into what you SHOULD be focusing on first if you want to create your Thought Leader Podcast. That focus should be: Creating a podcast that educates, engages and entices your ideal client to want to know more about you and how you can support them.

Introducing the:

PODCAST PROFIT FORMULA

$$S + T + U = I^3$$

Strategy + Tactic + U (YOU!) = Impact, Influence and Income.

Each of the elements in this formula has equal importance, because:

- Without a clear and/or correct strategy, you can end up with little to no outcome, especially if you don't know what that outcome is or how you're going to achieve that desired outcome.
- Without a clear and/or correct Tactic (which includes a compelling call to action) it can still take you much longer to achieve an outcome, if at all.
- Without defining U (YOU!), and what distinguishes you from hundreds of other podcasts, you can still get lost in the noise and struggle to be recognised as that go-to person and Industry Thought Leader.

The next three chapters will look more closely at each of the elements in the formula.

CHAPTER 3

STRATEGY

According to a recent Google search, a definition of 'strategy,' which I like and lean towards, is:

> **"…a plan of action designed to achieve
> a long-term or overall aim."**

When it comes to creating your Thought Leader Podcast – The Podcast Profit Framework (which I've followed for years with the thousands of podcasts I've produced) is *a plan of action, which is specifically designed to help you achieve your long-term or overall aim.*

PODCAST PROFIT FRAMEWORK

Produce Publish
Plan Promote
Purpose Profit

∿ Cut Through Noise ⊕ Expand Your Reach ⓢ Deepen Engagement

1) The Podcast Profit Framework: An Overview

The Podcast Profit Framework encompasses six sequential stages. It's important to complete each stage, along with all of the relevant components in that stage before moving on to the next.

Let's look at each of the stages, briefly:

a) Stage 1: Purpose

Why are you creating your podcast? Do you have a clear goal in mind? How will you leverage it to build influence, impact and income?

b) Stage 2: Plan

i) Your Podcast Creative Elements, which includes:

- Podcast Title
- Podcast Description, Keywords and Phrases
- Podcast Bio
- Podcast Introduction
- Podcast Outro
- Music Selection and Sound Effects (if any)
- Voiceover Professional (if any)

ii) Your Individual Episodes

- Who is your ideal client?
- What topics do they want to learn more about?
- How is your message going to cut through the noise?
- What format will enable you to engage with your listener from the introduction right through to your outro?

iii) Specific Strategy for Your Unique Situation

The specific outcome you want to achieve will determine the strategy you follow.

Here are some different outcomes, as an example:

- Strategy for an Author (or Aspiring Author)
- Strategy for a Speaker (or Aspiring Speaker)
- Strategy for Upselling Customers, i.e., Professional Accounting Firm
- Strategy for Raising Investor Capital for a Startup
- Strategy for Building Thought Leadership (Impact, Influence and Income)

c) Stage 3: Produce

Have you got a streamlined process in place that'll enable you to produce a professional and consistent on-brand message? Which tools will you use to record, edit/mix your audio?

d) Stage 4: Publish

What platform will you use to host your audio? Is free or paid a better option for you? [*] Is your podcast available on all major podcast including Apple, Android, Smart Speakers, and the Web?

[*] A word of caution if you're considering using a free hosting platform. How is that company funding their business and, more importantly, is there potential for that company to close down if they're unable to monetize their business? Sadly, I have heard of instances where companies have been unable to continue operations, which had artists and businesses desperately scrabbling

to download their podcasts before the site shut down and they lost all of their content.

Also, some hosting platform's business models may be to add advertisements to your show, something that as a Brand Strategist and business owner, I'm extremely wary of. Listeners may assume I endorse that company when clearly I haven't. It may even be a business that has different values from mine, so it may cause some confusion (and in some instances, criticism) from listeners. Therefore, be mindful when choosing a free vs. paid podcast host.

e) Stage 5: Promote

Do you have a clear strategy in place that has each of your podcast episodes being promoted and shared across various platforms? Are you keeping the content and creatives in line with what's typically expected from that platform?

f) Stage 6: Profit

Have you mapped out your Podcast Profit Pipeline (i.e. funnel)? And, do you have a process in place that will enable you to track, monitor and tweak as required, to ensure you're generating the best outcome? For instance, is your ideal client contacting you to find out more about how they can work with you? Remember, you can't improve something if you're not tracking and monitoring, so this is an ongoing important step.

===///===

While each of the six stages in The Podcast Profit Framework is important to position yourself as an Industry Thought Leader, the first two stages are critical. Hence, why I'm going to dive deeper into the first two stages of the Framework within this book, which is *Stage 1: Purpose* and *Stage 2: Plan*.

While we could spend time focusing on the ins and outs of technology, as I've mentioned earlier, you can have the best microphone and still struggle to become recognised as an Industry Thought Leader, while building influence, impact and income. However, I will provide you with a list of technologies I've used (and currently using) in the Produce, Publish, and Promote stages in Part 4, as well as keep an up to date list of technology on the private resources page, which is listed in the Addendum section of the book. So be sure to check there from time to time as well.

2) Podcast Profit Framework: Stage 1 – Purpose

Over the last year, I've spoken with a number of Change Makers and aspiring Thought Leaders who wanted to increase their reach and visibility with a podcast, which has been exciting.

What hasn't been exciting is realising they weren't ready. Yet. That's because they didn't have the right business model in place. You may be thinking: "What has business models got to do with launching a podcast?" It has everything to do with launching your podcast. Especially if you want to leverage your podcast to build influence, impact AND income. Because if you don't have the right business model (i.e. core business foundations) in place first, you'll be unable to leverage the numerous opportunities appropriately through all of the additional visibility and exposure your podcast will generate. Which was exactly what I recognised would happen with the Change Makers and aspiring Thought Leaders I was in conversation with.

They would have increased their visibility; however, they wouldn't have been able to leverage that additional exposure into leads, enquiries, and ultimately paying customers.

How about you? Have you got the right business foundations in place so that you can leverage the visibility your podcast will generate and nurture these into leads, enquiries and customers?

Let's step back for a moment to review a simplified business growth lesson. It's a culmination of what I've learned from mentors over the years as well as my own experience over the last two decades in business.

a) The Three Stages of Business Growth

1. Lean Stage: Your business is in start-up mode and you're building your core business foundations, systems, and processes.
2. Leverage Stage: You are leveraging the success you've generated in the Lean Stage growth of your business and continuing to build momentum as you scale your business.
3. Legacy Stage: You are implementing the strategies, systems and staff to set the business up for sale, or so you can step away from the business and it will continue to operate without you.

Three Stages of Business Growth

Lean Stage: Build Foundations	Leverage Stage: Build Momentum	Legacy Stage: Build Saleability
Create your Core Business Foundations: • Your Lucrative Niche • Your Signature Brand • Your Signature System • Your Signature Programs • Your Digital Assets (i.e. Irresistible Signature Giveaway, which could be your 3-Part Thought Leader Podcast Series)	Continue to build momentum to scale your business. This may include additional visibility tactics, systems and processes, highly skilled team, and automation as an example.	Continue to implement strategies, robust systems and staff to exit the business, whether through selling the business or hiring full time staff to take over the necessary day-to-day management and oversight of the business.

Sadly, many businesses focus on Stage 2: Leverage Stage: Building Momentum too soon, without first having built and strengthened their Core Business Foundations, systems and processes, which are required to build a sustainable and scalable business.

Any wonder businesses fail to build the traction they need to grow their businesses, even with the exposure they generate from their podcast. This is because they lack the Core Business Foundations and the required systems and processes needed. They end up riding the 'feast and famine' roller coaster, never quite reaching the level of freedom and lifestyle they desire.

Or, the opposite can occur. They grow their business to where they're unable to take on any additional clients due to their diaries being fully booked. In some cases they can end up despising the business they worked so hard to build. The freedom and lifestyle choices they dreamed their business would give them seem impossible to achieve.

I don't want either of these situations to happen to you, so let's take some time to review the Core Business Foundations to ensure you have these in place before you launch your podcast.

b) Lean Stage: Your Core Business Foundations

To recap, your Core Business Foundations include:

- Your Lucrative Niche
- Your Signature Brand
- Your Signature System
- Your Signature Programs
- Your Irresistible Signature Giveaway (which we'll work on in Chapter 4: Tactic: Your Thought Leader Podcast Series)

i) Your Lucrative Niche

Almost daily, I'm asked:

"How can I build a global audience?" "How can I get my message out on a global scale?" "How do I get more reach to make a bigger impact?"

My response?

"Speak to an audience of one. We get caught up focusing on the numbers. Size of our list; our social media connections; our podcast downloads, etc. While our goal may be to influence many people on a global scale, focusing only on 'vanity' numbers is not the best approach."

Instead, you should focus on:

- What keeps your ideal client up at night?
- What are his/her desires and dreams?
- And, what is the solution you offer to help him/her achieve her dream.

Then, craft a message that speaks hope and possibility into the conversations she's having with those around her and the conversation she has with herself, when no-one is around. When you do, she'll listen. She'll want to learn more from you. And, she'll reach out to you when you invite her to have a conversation.

Continue to do that. Every.Single.Day. Because when you get the message right, that audience of one WILL expand. Globally. So, focus on your audience of one, because that's what making a difference one message at a time and one person at a time truly means.

A great success story of tapping into a lucrative niche was one I heard of many years ago, where a newly graduated dentist decided to niche into paediatric dentistry. As he continued to specialise in this area, it wasn't long before a number of his colleagues and even other dentists across the country began to hear about the successes he was having with his young patients. They began to refer more difficult cases to him. He soon had a fully booked client list, with parents flying their children across the country for a consultation. The growth of his business meant he had to hire additional specialists, all because he decided to niche and specialise in a specific area.

That's what specialisation and tapping into a lucrative niche can generate for your business too.

Complete the following exercise as you continue to define your lucrative niche:

- What problems does he/she typically have? And, what are the words and phrases he/she uses to describe their problems?
- What does your ideal client seek? Desire? Want? And, what words does he/she use to describe what he/she wants?
- How can you support him/her in overcoming his/her problems? What results will he/she achieve through working with you?
- Can you narrow down even further and target an even smaller niche?
- How highly do the people in your proposed niche rank solving their problem?

On a scale of 1-10, the people within your niche must rank solving this problem a SIX or higher to make your niche viable for you. Be honest when answering this question.

- Is your proposed niche large enough to be viable for your business?
- Is the general 'culture' of your proposed niche open to making a change?

Some niches have such a strong culture that it makes it almost impossible for them to break the barriers. To them it seems to go against the ethos of their industry. Any time your niche is not open to making a change will mean you'll often find marketing and making sales difficult, time consuming and costly.

Yes | No

- Do the people within your niche have a history of investing in things of a similar (or complementary) nature to what you offer?

Yes | No If yes, in what typically are they investing? Can you do/offer something unique/different that gives an even better and/or innovative solution to your ideal client's issue?

- Are they easy to find? Where will you find them?
- Do you enjoy working with them?

If you can't answer these with total clarity, then I encourage you to do some more research into your ideal client/lucrative niche.

ii) Your Signature Brand

Many people mistakenly believe their brand is their business cards, their website, and letterhead, etc. These are all important; however, they are (what I like to call) your 'brand touch points'. They bring your Signature Brand to life, by exuding your brand's core values and, ultimately, the experience you want to create.

When referring to your 'brand,' I'm talking about your reputation. It's the perception others have of you. It's what they think about you, and what they say about you when your name is mentioned. In fact, helping my clients get totally clear on their Signature Brand (and an aspect of their Signature Brand, which I call 'Your Inner Brilliance') is something I love to do. Because it's not just my ideal client's brand message, voice, approach, and what will help him/her truly differentiate himself/herself in the marketplace. It's MUCH more than that. It's getting total clarity on her gifts and her purpose. Because her deepest desire is not just to create a successful business. That actually comes as a result of her doing great work and clients investing in her services. It's much deeper than that. She's here to make a difference. A REAL difference. And, helping her clarify what that is, with just the right words - not just any words, but THE words that depict WHO she is, and WHAT she's here to champion through her work - is why I do what I do!

During one of my Signature Brand VIP Day's with a client, not only did I have goosebumps when we captured the words for her Inner Brilliance statement and brand foundations - I also got goosebumps when we mapped out her business model. This can often happen once we capture a client's Inner Brilliance statement. I begin to see how that will come to fruition through her business model and unique offerings. It's in those moments I literally get goosebumps. When I do, I know she's on track!

Defining your Signature Brand is vital if you want to stand out in the crowd, especially for Change Makers and aspiring Thought Leaders.

We'll dive much deeper into Your Signature Brand in the section of U [YOU!] as we explore: The Distinction Triad and guide you with some key questions to help you define Your Thought Leadership Brand as well as your Thought Leadership Core Message. However, for now, let's define your Brand Attributes, Brand Strengths and Core Values.

Define your Signature Brand Attributes:

Your brand attributes include your unique characteristics and qualities, as well as any unique quirky aspects of your personality that make you – YOU!

- List 5-6 features and/or qualities that you would say are unique about you. (If you get stuck, go to our Resources page and download the Brand Attributes Quiz).
- What do people constantly admire and say about you?
- Do you have a quirkiness about you that is often mentioned as being essentially 'you'?

For instance, one of my colleagues has a whacky sense of humour and you just know you're going to have one of those deep belly laughs when you're in his presence. For him, humour, laughter and fun are all important so he incorporates all three things within the unique experience he creates for his community and his clients.

Another one of my colleagues is a former musician with music very much still an important part of his life. It's not unusual for him to reference lyrics of a song as part of his story telling, or for him to burst into a song to lighten up the mood. So, this is very much part of who he is and what he continues to create as an experience for his clients and community. A suggestion I made was for him to incorporate musical terms and references within his program titles and throughout his copy where appropriate, which would be unique and distinguishable from everyone else who was offering similar services.

Define your Signature Brand Strengths:

Your brand strengths are your gifts and talents; the skills and abilities that come naturally to you. This can often be difficult to clarify with certainty and confidence because so many of us take our strengths for granted.

I've thought long and hard about why this may be, and over the years I've come to believe that it's because our strengths come so naturally to us we assume anyone can do it. Which is far from the truth. For example, my mother has always loved networking and talking to people. She is an extrovert through and through and loves interacting with people. One of the things she continued to do well into her 90s was to visit elderly people in a Hostel that was located very close to her home. The elderly people she visited were extremely frail (some much younger than she was) and due to their ailments were unable to go out. By visiting them, spending time with them, and listening to their stories (for the hundredth time in some cases), my mother helped them feel special, because here was someone who was taking time out of her day to sit and listen to them.

However, if you were to ask my mother to list some of her strengths, she would never in a million years have recognised that this was a unique strength, nor that she was making a difference in the lives of others.

I wonder, how many of your unique strengths do you take for granted? Write down all of your strengths - those things that come naturally and that you do well. Don't disregard anything.

These questions/statements may help you:

- What are 5 or 6 strengths that come naturally for you? (If you get stuck, complete the '3 Situations' exercise below.)
- What do people most admire about you? What are people regularly saying that you do well and they wish they could do?
- Exercise: Think about 3 Situations where you had to overcome a challenge and/or problem that you were able to resolve to a successful outcome. What strengths and skills did you use to secure these outcomes?

  You can follow these questions to help you:

    - What problem/situation were you confronted with?
    - How were you able to fix this problem/situation? What actions did you take? [*]
    - What was the outcome due to you taking action?

  [*] HOW you addressed the problem/situation and the actions you took are evidence of the strengths and skills you have. You'll most likely find a common theme in the strengths and skills you used to overcome the problem/situation.

Define Your Signature Brand Core Values:

Your Signature Brand Core Values are ideals, standard and beliefs, which define who you are, and what you stand for.

- Go through the Signature Brand Core Values (below) and select 5-6 core values that resonate the most with you.

   Note: When taking my clients through this process, sometimes they can struggle to narrow it down to just 5-6 values. If this sounds like you, here are the steps I encourage them to do:

   - Go through the entire list and tick anything that stands out.
   - Go back over the list and ask: 'Is this a MUST-have value?' If it's not of significant importance, cross it out.
   - Some core values will be similar to others. Compare the words, and select and highlight the 'one' core value that resonates with you the most.
   - Go through this process until you are left with 5-6 core values.

Signature Brand Core Values

Abundance	Acceptance	Accountability	Achievement
Advancement	Adventure	Advocacy	Ambition
Appreciation	Attractiveness	Autonomy	Balance
Being the Best	Boldness	Brilliance	Calmness
Caring	Challenge	Charity	Cheerfulness
Cleverness	Community	Commitment	Compassion

Cooperation	Collaboration	Consistency	Contribution
Creativity	Credibility	Curiosity	Daring
Decisiveness	Dedication	Dependability	Diversity
Empathy	Encouragement	Enthusiasm	Ethics
Excellence	Expressiveness	Faith	Family
Friendships	Flexibility	Freedom	Fun
Generosity	Grace	Growth	Flexibility
Happiness	Health	Honesty	Humility
Humour	Inclusiveness	Independence	Individuality
Innovation	Inspiration	Intelligence	Intuition
Joy	Kindness	Knowledge	Leadership
Learning	Love	Loyalty	Making a Difference
Mindfulness	Motivation	Optimism	Open-Mindedness
Originality	Passion	Performance	Personal Development
Proactive	Professionalism	Quality	Recognition
Risk Taking	Safety	Security	Service
Spirituality	Stability	Peace	Perfection
Playfulness	Popularity	Power	Recognition
Proactivity	Professionalism	Punctuality	Preparedness
Relationships	Reliability	Resilience	Resourcefulness
Responsibility	Responsiveness	Security	Self-Control
Selflessness	Simplicity	Stability	Success
Teamwork	Thankfulness	Thoughtfulness	Traditionalism
Trustworthiness	Understanding	Uniqueness	Usefulness
Versatility	Vision	Warmth	Wealth
Well-Being	Wisdom	Zeal	

iii) Your Signature System

Your Signature System is your Intellectual Property. It's the steps you take your clients through to take them from where they are stuck to where they want to be.

It captures your expertise into a step-by-step unique, proven system.

To help you create your Signature System, let me share one of mine, as an example. Let's look at my work helping Change Makers and aspiring Thought Leaders go from Invisible to Influential (and profitable) with a Podcast.

Here's my Signature System for my Podcasting with Purpose offerings:

PODCASTING WITH PURPOSE
SIGNATURE SYSTEM

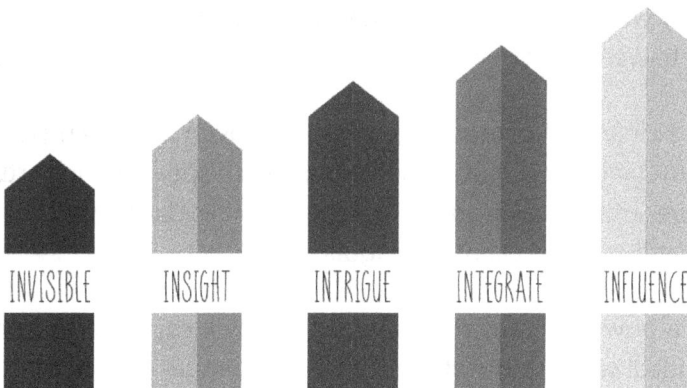

INVISIBLE   INSIGHT   INTRIGUE   INTEGRATE   INFLUENCE

Step 1: Invisible

My clients will often say: "I feel like the world's best kept secret. I have so much to offer; however, hardly anyone knows about me," which is one of the reasons they reach out for my support. They have a level of knowledge and experience that's valuable and can make an impact in the lives of their clients, however hardly anyone knows about them.

Step 2: Insight

In this step of my Signature System, I take my clients through a number of assessments and activities to help them get clear on their unique Signature Brand (i.e. their Inner Brilliance), their Vision and Mission, and unique voice. If they aren't clear in any area of their Core Business Foundations, we'll work on it together until they are confident and excited in what they have to offer.

Step 3: Intrigue

The next step is getting totally clear on their ideal client. As well as the key words and phrases that will engage and entice their ideal client to want to learn more about them and the work they're doing.

With a clear and compelling message woven into each podcast, each message, each social media post, each speaking opportunity and presentation, will ensure my client speaks directly to the heart of what their ideal client is struggling with.

With a powerful consistent message, they'll continue to intrigue their ideal client so they'll want to listen to more of their podcasts.

Step 4: Integrate

Without an integrated approach business owners will often feel like they're spinning their wheels, stretching themselves too thin with all of the marketing they're doing. Nothing is building any traction so they end up giving up.

This is another vital step where I help clients define their Podcast Profit Pipeline, along with an integrated marketing approach to give them the best chance at building momentum. Everything they do continues to engage, educate and entice their ideal client through their Podcast Profit Pipeline.

Step 5: Influence

With all of the other steps in place, every single touch point my clients has in place continues to nurture their ideal client to the point where they want to find out how to work with them. I follow the exact steps with all of my marketing, my podcasts and the content I share, which is why I'll so often receive comments like:

"I've learned SO much from you. How can I work with you?" "I need to work with you – when can we speak?" "We need to talk…"

This is what my Signature System helps my clients achieve. Let's map out yours with these three simple questions.

1. What's ONE major problem your ideal client is struggling with and what is the outcome they want to achieve?

2. Think about the outcome they want to achieve and how you're able to leverage your expertise to help them. Then ask yourself:

- ○ What's the first step they'll need to take? Write it down
- ○ What's the next step they'll need to take? Write it down.
- ○ What's the next step they'll need to take? Write it down.
- ○ What's the next step they'll need to take? Write it down.
- ○ What's the next step they'll need to take? Write it down.

You see where I'm going with this?

3. Typically you want between 5 to 7 steps (maximum). If you have more steps in your initial draft, see which steps can be put together and refine your Signature System down to between 5 to 7 steps.

Give each step an outcome-focused heading; add a few benefit-driven bullet points and you're set to go.

iv) Your Signature Programs

Your Signature Programs is a menu of offerings with different investment levels.

Each Signature Program incorporates elements of your Signature System. Most times, the higher the level of investment, the more time you will typically have to spend with them, or do a lot more for them.

To help you get your creative juices flowing, let's review my three offerings with Podcasting with Purpose.

1. DIY – Do It Yourself Signature Program

These include my Podcasting with Purpose and Interviewing with Purpose Self-Paced Online Programs. I've put all of my knowledge into video trainings, along with templates, checklists and workbooks into online training, which clients can access and study at their own pace.

2. DWY – Done With You Signature Program

This is my Podcast Profit Platform Program, which includes everything a client needs to take them from Invisible to Influential and profitable, with my team and I supporting them every step of the way and doing the post-production, publishing and promotion for them.

It includes their own Podcast Platform on our Ambitious Entrepreneur Podcast Network, editing and production of their podcasts, and promotion of their podcasts. We even include ongoing monthly trainings (across key areas of business growth), in-person masterminds, while being part of a community of Change Makers who are changing the world with their message.

This is our high-end, high touch program and also includes access to our online trainings as well as their own customized 3-part

Thought Leader Podcast Series, which they will use as part of their Podcast Profit Pipeline.

3. DFY – Done For You Signature Program

This is our Thought Leader Podcast Series offering and is specifically for clients who want a podcast series to build their influence, their list and their leads, but do not want an ongoing podcast.

My team and I do everything for them, including pre- and post-audio production, publishing and promotion of each episode. We even provide a Podcast Interviewer where we interview our clients. In fact, we hold their hand – every step of the way and can even create their website squeeze pages and their follow-up nurturing emails. All they need to do is step up to the microphone to share their expertise.

Over to you.

Here are three questions to begin mapping out your Signature Program(s):

1. What needs to be covered in your program? Typically working on ONE outcome is a great guideline so as not to overwhelm your client. Remember: You don't need to put everything into your program, unless this is a 12-month high touch program.
2. Is it a Do-It-Yourself (DIY), Done-With-You (DWY), or Done-For-You (DFY) offering?
3. How will the program be structured? For instance:

   a. Will it be in-person, online, or a combination of both?
   b. Will it start off with a VIP Day/session where you get to work together on a specific area with your client, with subsequent follow-up sessions

3. Over what time frame will you be working with clients?
4. Are you including worksheets, recordings and done-for-you templates, etc. to build additional value for your clients?
5. What price point will each of your Signature Programs be price at?

**Get into Action – Stage 1: Purpose:
Your Core Business Foundations**

- Define your Lucrative Niche
- Define your Signature Brand
- Define your Signature System
- Create your Signature Programs

---

3) The Podcast Profit Framework: Stage 2 - Plan Your Podcast Creatives

Now is the time to leverage the information you've identified as part of your Signature Brand to guide you in the planning and creation of your podcast creatives.

Note: I would encourage you to read and work through the exercises in Chapter 5: U [YOU!] first, before you finalise your creative elements. This will help you bring your brand message to life.

a) Your Podcast Title

This is the name of your podcast.

Here are some suggestions and examples to guide you.

Your podcast title incorporates the name of your business/ organization.

- Example: Business Women Australia Podcast

Business Women Australia's intention was to create a podcast platform where their Premier and Diamond Members could showcase their expertise.

Outcome-Focused Podcast Title:

- Example: Speaker Success Podcast

Women Speakers Association wanted to build a podcast platform where they could showcase their Premier members and Alliance Partners. Information shared on the show continues to support members in growing their business through speaking. Their members want to become successful speakers and therefore the title of the podcast was centred on what they knew their members were interested in and would benefit from.

A Podcast Title that is targeted to whom the podcast is for and about:

- Example: Women In Leadership Podcast

This is one of my own podcasts and focuses specifically on women in leadership, whether they lead a team within their own business or within a corporate setting. I want to make sure people know exactly what the podcast is about as well as be easy to find as women search for podcasts on women in leadership.

- Example: The Christian Entrepreneurs Podcast

This is another one of my podcasts, which is business focused, however specifically for faith-based entrepreneurs.

- Example: Ambitious Entrepreneur Show

Previously titled 'Business Success Podcast', I changed the name to Ambitious Entrepreneur Show to focus specifically on entrepreneurs and business owners – who are driven and passionate about growing a successful and impactful business.

As a side note, Ambitious Entrepreneur Show and The Ambitious Entrepreneur Podcast Network (my Podcast Production Company) has that name as it aligns with the blend of our Brand Archetypes: Teacher, Ruler, and Explorer. [For those of you who are in my Podcasting with Purpose Program, or any of my programs for that matter, you will know exactly what I mean as you would have discovered what your Brand Archetypes are as well].

Whatever title you select for your podcast, ensure it's purposeful, intentional and on-brand. I caution you not to opt for creative titles that are ambiguous and confusing as they are not the best approach when it comes to a Thought Leader Podcast. Unless of course ambiguity is what you are looking for and specific to your brand.

b) Your Podcast Description, Keywords and Phrases

The reader (or listener) should instantly be able to discern who your podcast is for, what it is about, and the benefit and value they'll receive through listening to it. A clear, concise and outcome focused paragraph that's relevant to your ideal client is what you should aim for.

Here is an overview of each of the descriptions of the podcasts listed above to help you get your creative juices flowing:

- Business Women Australia Podcast

Hosted by Annemarie Cross – Business Women Australia Podcast is a bi-monthly podcast for ambitious women who are serious about business success and leadership development, and interested in building their knowledge and skills.

- Speaker Success Podcast

Speaker Success Podcast is a collaboration between Women Speakers Association and the Ambitious Entrepreneur Podcast Network. A bi-monthly podcast, which features inspiring women with a bold vision who are sharing their powerful insights, to help other business women use speaking to build a thriving business.

- Women In Leadership Podcast

Women In Leadership Podcast – *THE podcast that empowers women to achieve their full potential whether they are in corporate or working in their own business.*

Guests will share the highs and lows of their careers, the challenges they had to face head-on, as well as their words of wisdom to help us become more purposeful in all aspects of our lives, our businesses and our careers.

- The Christian Entrepreneurs Podcast

Welcome to The Christian Entrepreneurs' Podcast.

Conversations with Christian Entrepreneurs to inspire and empower Christian Business Owners to walk strongly in their faith, while building a thriving business that honours Him, in every way.

- Ambitious Entrepreneur Show

Are you struggling to stand out in a crowded market place, get more clients, and turning a prospect into a customer – a customer who pays you what you're worth? Building the business of your dreams, and doing what you love does not have to be hard, frustrating, and exhausting IF you know the RIGHT steps!

Annemarie and her guests will show you how to navigate and stand out in a rapidly-changing and competitive marketplace so you become an influential voice in your field.

c) Your Podcast Bio (for you as the Host)

A concise, outcome-focused bio is key.

Here's mine as an example to help you begin crafting yours:

Annemarie Cross - Founder of Podcasting with Purpose Podcast Training and Production Agency is an Award-winning Podcast Host and Producer.

Dubbed 'The Podcasting Queen' by her community, she is recognised as a pioneer in this space, after starting her first podcast in 2008.

Combining her love of technology, branding and digital media, she's been able to build a business, client base, and support team that is truly global by harnessing the power of social media and online technologies – particularly podcasting. She now supports Change Makers and aspiring Thought Leaders to cut through the noise and go From Invisible to Influential and profitable with her Done-With-You Podcast Platform and/or Done-For You Podcast Series.

d) Your Podcast Introduction

I've always gone the route of:

Tell them what they're going to get out of investing their valuable time in listening to your podcast – right at the beginning of your podcast. I do this with the pre-recorded intro, where I typically use a professional voiceover artist, followed by a tailored introduction of the specific content that will be covered, along with the guest I'll be interviewing for that episode, which I read out as the host.

While I do make mention of the show sponsor, for a majority of my shows, I will have no rambling or banter about what I did on the weekend, just the content my guest will be speaking about and the benefits listeners will gain through listening to the show. I assume my listeners are like me. They are busy and appreciate me getting straight to the point! [This is based on feedback from hundreds of business owners as well].

Note: You know your audience best. So, have fun as you continue to create your intros and outros. Remember, nothing is set in stone. Typically, the deeper the relationship you have with someone, the more likely they'll listen to you as you share some of your personal involvements. So a balanced approach is often the best approach.

Whatever your point is – get to it as efficiently and effectively as possible. [I remember listening to one podcast host who took over 30 minutes to answer a question I'm sure could have been answered in 5 minutes. Thank goodness for the double speed listening option].

The rule is, there are no rules. Just what works best for you and your audience. So, if you've tried something for a while and you want to change it up – go for it.

Here's an overview of each of the intros and outros for each of the podcasts listed previously to help guide you.

Example: Business Women Australia

Pre-recorded Intro:

"Welcome to Business Women Australia Podcast. The podcast for ambitious women who are serious about business success and leadership development, keen to increase their knowledge and skills."

Followed by the tailored introduction where I come in with the specific content we'll be covering for that episode:

"Welcome to [Business Women Australia Podcast] - episode 23. I'm your Host Annemarie Cross - The Podcasting Queen and Founder of PodcastingWithPurpose.com podcast training.

My guest today has a question for you: "What are you doing today to proactively move towards achieving your dreams?"

Joining me on today's show is Suzzanne Laidlaw.

Suzzanne has over 25 years in key business management roles and has started and built many businesses from the ground up. She inspires individuals and business owners to reach their potential and be the best versions of themselves they can be.

Having faced & overcome adversity many times, including saving her husband from a house fire and overcoming a life-threatening disease, she understands how to overcome set-backs. If you're looking for businesses or personal growth or want to know the key to planning and sticking to your goals, she can help you.

On today's show, Suzzanne will share:

- How to identify your business objectives and learn the 'How, When & Why's' of planning;
- Find out how to increase profits and improve cash flow through simple but effective accounting techniques;
- Understand what sets apart those who are successful in business and those who are not."

Welcome to the show, Suzzanne.

Example: Speaker Success Podcast

Pre-recorded Intro:

"Inspiring Women, Bold Vision, and Powerful Insights to help you use speaking to build a thriving business. This is Speakers Success Podcast brought to you by Women Speakers Association. Now for today's show."

Followed by the tailored introduction where I come in with the specific content we'll be covering in that episode:

"Welcome to another episode of Speakers Success Podcast. I'm your Host – Annemarie Cross, the Podcasting Queen, Founder of PodcastingWithPurpose.com Podcast Training.

Thinking about writing a book, however, you're not sure on the pros and cons of self-publishing, traditional publishing, or hybrid publishing? In fact, what is hybrid publishing anyway? Today's guest is going to answer that as well as how we can save time and money by avoiding some of the common mistakes authors make.

Joining me on today's show is Karen Strauss.

Karen is a Book Publishing veteran with over 30 years of experience working with well-known celebrities such as Martha Stewart and George Will as well as many Speakers, entrepreneurs, and authors who are writing books to get their message heard.

She has worked at major publishers such as Random House, Crown and Macmillan and in 2011 founded Hybrid Global Publishing for independent authors looking for a traditional publishing experience coupled with a highly modern approach to promotion and marketing.

On today's show, Karen will share:

- Top 10 Mistakes Authors make and how to avoid them;
- How to decide which publishing option is right for you;
- How a book will benefit you as a Speaker and entrepreneur.

Example: Women in Leadership Podcast

Pre-recorded Intro:

"Welcome to Women in Leadership Podcast featuring success insights from women around the globe. Now over to our host – Annemarie Cross."

Followed by the tailored introduction where I come in with the specific content for that episode:

Welcome to Women in Leadership Podcast - episode 100 brought to you by Podcasting with Purpose – helping you stand out, be heard and become an influential voice in your industry with a podcast. I'm your host, Annemarie Cross - The Podcasting Queen.

According to my guest today, fifty per cent of Australian women in business aren't paying themselves. And, she's on a mission to help women gain an understanding of what's happening with their finances, why they must value themselves and the important role they play in their business, so they can!

Joining me on today's show is Peace Mitchell.

Peace is the co-founder of AusMumpreneur, Australia's #1 community for mums in business, and the Women's Business School, which provides flexible & time efficient business education for women who've started their own business.

On today's show Peace is going to share:

- Your business should be your best friend. It's not success if you're working 70 hours a week and never seeing your family, exercising, or doing things you enjoy.
- The importance of understanding your numbers and paying attention to what's happening with your figures.
- Why you must surround yourself with great people. We're taught in school to do things by ourselves and not ask for help, but when it comes to business you can't do it all by yourself.

Example: The Christian Entrepreneurs Podcast

Pre-recorded Intro:

"Welcome to The Christian Entrepreneurs Podcast - Conversations with Christian Entrepreneurs to inspire and empower Christian Business Owners to walk strongly in their faith, WHILE building a thriving business that honours Him, in every way. Now over to your host – Annemarie Cross."

Followed by the tailored introduction where I come in with the specific content for that episode:

"Welcome to The Christian Entrepreneurs Podcast - episode 84 brought to you by Podcasting with Purpose – helping you stand out, be heard and become an influential voice in your industry with a podcast. I'm your host, Annemarie Cross - The Podcasting Queen.

Today's guest says: "Remember that your Visions are greater than your fear and your actions are the evidence of your faith. So show up and keep shining, because you were made for a purpose and the world needs you."

Joining me today is Fideliz Cruz.

Fideliz is passionate about making women feel their best, by helping them bring out their uniqueness and authenticity through Life Coaching. It is her vision to see women rise up in leadership in any aspect of their lives, using their gifts and talents to build a life that they love.

Fideliz is the founder of Kingdom Women Entrepreneur. A sisterhood community for faith-filled entrepreneurs created for equipping and support in the areas of business as well as faith walk.

On today's show, Fideliz is going to share:

- Always seek for Godly Wisdom. Enquiring of God not just in our personal lives but in ALL aspects of our lives, particularly in business;
- Remember that we are stewards of God's gifts and talents. Everything we have comes from Him;
- Everything starts with a Vision. Start with the end in mind and know that each step is directed and ordered by the Lord."

Example: Ambitious Entrepreneur Show

Pre-recorded Intro:

"You're listening to the Award-Winning Podcast – the Ambitious Entrepreneur Show. Featuring business experts, industry disruptors, game changers, and thought leaders to help you navigate a constantly changing marketplace. Want to build a successful business and become an influential voice in your industry? The Ambitious Entrepreneur Show will show you how. Now, over to your host – Annemarie Cross."

Followed by the tailored introduction where I come in with the specific content for that episode:

"Welcome to the Ambitious Entrepreneurs Podcast - episode 202 brought to you by Podcasting with Purpose – helping you stand out, be heard and become an influential voice in your industry with a podcast. I'm your host, Annemarie Cross - The Podcasting Queen.

Selling is something many service-based ambitious entrepreneurs struggle with. Imagine if you could follow a breakthrough sales system that took the focus off of having to sell yourself: It not only shortened the sales cycle, but also it delivered sales conversation rates as high as 94%. Would you be interested in learning more? I know I certainly would.

Joining me on today's show is Steve Brossman.

Steve is the Amazon Best Selling Author of the Book, *Stand Up Stand Out or Stand Aside*, a Blueprint for creating your Authority Factor.

He is the Creator of the Authority Sales Blueprint a breakthrough system that is helping professionals stand out in crowded markets, avoid the price wars and makes selling faster and more enjoyable.

On today's show, Steve is going to share:

1. How to quickly position yourself as a leader in your market so you can attract more high level clients.
2. A breakthrough sales system that takes the focus off selling yourself, shortens the sales process and creates conversion rates that have reached as high as 94%.
3. A proven way that professional service providers can package their services and easily sell them for higher prices."

e) Your Podcast Outro

I have a pre-recorded outro that I play at the end of the show after my guest and I finish talking. It has the exact same music as the intro, and often ties the show's overall theme with a call to action that encourages listeners to access a resource I know will be valuable for them.

I typically end the show with a guest by re-iterating a few of the main points that was shared, as well as repeating how listeners can find out more about the guest, and then end the show with the pre-recorded outro.

Again, you may have a number of different pre-recorded outros that you'll use to align with a specific marketing campaign you're launching. Or, you may like to change it up every few shows so that listeners don't become bored hearing the same message and switch off.

Here are some examples to help you get your creative juices flowing when creating your outro:

Pre-Recorded Outro – Speakers Success Podcast:

With the Call to Action to access their free opt-in:

"You've been listening to Speakers Success Podcast, brought to you by Women's Speakers Association. If you're ready to share your message in a bigger way so you can build a thriving business, get your free Speakers Success Plan at SpeakerSuccessGift.com."

Note: We've recently discussed me mentioning the free opt-in gift as a reminder to listeners who haven't yet accessed it. We'll do this and see if we can get an increase in the number of people who sign up for the gift.

Pre-Recorded Outro – The Christian Entrepreneurs Podcast:

With the Call to Action to access the free opt-in:

"You've been listening to the The Christian Entrepreneurs Podcast, brought to you by PodcastingWithPurpose.com – Stand Out, Be Heard - INFLUENCE. Want to influence change with your own podcast? Access our free podcast training including our no-cost and low-cost tools to get you started at www.PodcastingWithPurpose.com/minitraining that's www.PodcastingWithPurpose.com/minitraining."

Pre-Recorded Outro – Women in Leadership Podcast:

With the Call to Action to join the BEtheDifferenceMovement/Community:

"You've been listening to Women in Leadership Podcast – brought to you by BeTheDifferenceMovement.com – Changing the World, one message at a time. Do you feel called to influence REAL change with your message? Join our supportive community of like-minded influencers, thought leaders, and disruptors – at: www.BeTheDifferencemovement.com that's BeTheDifferencemovement.com"

f)   Music Selection and Sound Effects (if any)

Every single touch point that relates to your podcast, speaks your brand. This is true for your music. Is your intro music, voiceover professional (if you use one), and sound effects on-brand and creating the experience you want to create for your listeners? Do they reflect the experience you want to create? Or does it put them off?

Each of these elements, when selected with purpose and intention, creates a unique and powerful experience for your audience. An experience which will both engage and entice a person to continue listening. Or not. With only seconds to capture someone's attention, when it comes to your music selection ensure you consider:

- Tempo
- Mood
- Genre

The experience you want to create for your listener should impact your selection of music. This is why I'll often spend time listening to dozens (and dozens) of musical scores until I find THE one that perfectly depicts my client and the experience they want to create. In fact, I can sense within the first few opening bars whether it's a good fit or not.

As business owners, the external elements/touch points that expresses our brand and the experience/reputation we want to create, is key. The first step is to look at the core values and experience you've documented that you want to create when it comes to your podcast and then to search for music, sound effects and voiceover professionals that exude that experience.

Refer to the Tools and Resources section for the resources I use for music and sound effects.

g) Voiceover Professional (if any)

Similarly with a voiceover professional, you want their tone of voice, pacing, and emphasis of certain words and phrases in your introduction and outro to speak your brand. Be clear on the core values and experience you want to create with your podcast and find a voiceover professional whose voice depicts that.

When you approach him/her, ensure you document exactly what you want so he/she is clear. Don't get caught out – like I have. One time, I forgot to spell out the pronunciation of a specific word. Subsequently, the voiceover professional I hired got the pronunciation wrong. Because it was something quite easy to mix up, the buck stopped with me. I had to get it re-recorded at my own expense, which I was happy to do, since I didn't take the time to iterate that clearly in the first place, which in hindsight I should have done.

Refer to the Tools and Resources section for the resources I use when looking for voiceover professionals.

> **Get into Action: Stage 2: Plan Your Podcast Creatives**
>
> - Define your Podcast Title
> - Define your Podcast Description, Keywords and Phrases
> - Create your Podcast Host Bio
> - Create your Podcast Introduction and Outro
> - Select Music and Sound Effects
> - Select Voiceover Professional

4) The Podcast Profit Framework: Stage 2 – Plan Your Individual Episodes

Each time I plan a show, there are a number of things I always consider. These include:

- What are the challenges and issues my ideal client is dealing with and is seeking to learn more about?
- What specific topic is going to be valuable for my ideal client, in terms of education and inspiration, that is relevant to these challenges and issues?
- What are some unique angles that can be brought to the conversation to add even more value to my ideal client, and the challenges and issues they face? For instance, helping them overcome their issues more quickly, less expensive, following a suggested step-by-step plan, etc.?

I have created a streamlined process of gathering information from my guests. We have streamlined our processes and systems to a point where I now have an entire team who handles all of this for me. In fact, it has worked so well for me that I'm now giving all of my clients who go through my online Podcasting with Purpose Training access to everything I use, so they don't have to reinvent the wheel.

The following outline gives you an example of a show structure I'll often use that will ensure you capture and maintain your listeners' attention throughout the show.

[Note, the two podcast episodes that were nominated for the Best Business Podcast Award, with one going on to win the award, followed this structure. This still remains a structure I follow with most of my podcast episodes].

- The introduction;
- The hook, which will capture the audience's attention from the outset;
- Validate your guest, with a selection of relevant achievements and three key points he/she will cover on the show;
- The show itself:
  - Set up the show and why this is this relevant NOW for listeners;
  - A few pertinent key statistics and validation content;
  - This section dives deeper into the 'How tos' of the three key points you mentioned in your introduction;
  - Wrap up the show;
  - Further information about how people can connect with the guest;
- The outro and Call to Action.

> **Get into Action: Stage 2: Plan Your Individual Episode**
>
> • Map out your Podcast Episode Format

5) The Podcast Profit Framework: Stage 2 - Plan Your Specific Strategy for Your Unique Situation

Your overall goal for your podcast will determine the steps you'll take to achieve your desired outcome.

Note: In most of the following examples I assume you have your Core Business Foundations in place and are clear on your business model (i.e. how you're going to generate income), including:

- Your Lucrative Niche
- Your Signature Brand
- Your Signature System
- Your Signature Programs
- Your Irresistible Signature Giveaway

If not, I highly recommend you get clear on these first, otherwise no amount of publicity with your podcast is going to generate the impact, influence and income you desire.

If this is an area you're struggling with and you want further support and hand holding, refer to the Addendum 2: How to Work with Annemarie Cross (at the back of the book) and consider joining my Money, Marketing, and Mindset Mastermind to help you get these Core Business Foundations in place first. Or, my Core Business Foundations Course.

a) Example: If You Are an Author (or Aspiring Author)

Ultimate goal: To showcase your expertise and upsell to higher-level programs using your book as a credibility-building tool, and your podcast to nurture and strengthen your relationship with listeners (i.e. your ideal client). Leverage your book to get you opportunities to speak on stage, and/or the media including other podcasts. Create a 3-part Thought Leader Podcast Series and use that as you call to action. You'll be surprised how many people will build 'know, like and trust' more rapidly with you by listening to your podcast series, than if they are just reading your book.

When reading content, people will often bring their own perceptions to the conversation, or won't get a true sense of what you were trying to portray if they just scan quickly through the pages. A podcast, however, will enable you to deepen engagement with your listener through the tone of your voice and the overall experience you create.

Reading 'LOL' versus hearing someone laugh out loud is a completely different experience. I'll often find myself laughing alongside the person who is laughing, especially if they have one of those hilariously infectious laughs that can have you snort out loud if you're not careful! [I've nearly done that a few times while commuting by train and catching up on some of my favourite podcasts]. Consider adding a few chapters of your book along with worksheets for people to deepen their learning alongside your podcast series.

For aspiring Authors who have not yet written their book, consider following the steps, which I have taken in the creation of this book:

- Use your Signature System, with each step becoming a chapter, or sub-chapter of your book.
- Interview other Industry Thought Leaders and incorporate their insights and successes into your book to validate what you are saying or to bring another valuable viewpoint to the conversation.
- Repurpose articles and social media posts and incorporate where relevant into your chapters and sub-chapters.
- Consider doing an ongoing podcast series that is aligned with your book title, with the call to action leading back to, either:
  - Your Irresistible Signature Giveaway, which incorporates a few chapters of your book along with your Thought Leader Podcast Series.
  - Your book's sales page.

Personally, I would lead people back to your Irresistible Signature Giveaway so you can build your list and begin nurturing and building 'know, like and trust.'

b) Example: If You Are a Speaker (or Aspiring Speaker)

Ultimate goal: To showcase your expertise and engaging style to secure speaking opportunities.

Note: You have two desired outcomes when it comes to being a speaker.

One: To impress and get a 'YES!' from conference organisers and event planners (people who have the authority to make a decision to hire and/or invite you to speak).

Two: To impress and get a 'YES!' from event attendees to your Call to Action.

Both require a different approach.

Event Coordinators are extremely busy and typically won't have a lot of time to spend listening to a podcast or a Thought Leader Podcast Series. However, if you're building your Thought Leadership with videos of you speaking on other stages, an overview of what you can offer their audience, and the benefits of them hiring you as a speaker, then incorporating a few podcast episodes into your overall strategy where they can see the topics you cover and the value you bring, could be beneficial.

Conference and Event attendees are an entirely different matter, however. Incorporating a podcast series where people can access even more information is a great way to build your list and begin nurturing your relationship with people in the audience who have only just heard about you and are therefore not yet in a position to invest with you.

You can consider saying something like this at the end of your presentation:

"I've only just scratched the surface today and I know for a number of you here, you're ready to take what you've learned to an even greater level. Go ahead and access my Podcast Series at [link] where I go into each area even further, while also covering more points, which I didn't have time to go in to today."

Of course you'll have your back of the room products and other offerings, however, as mentioned, your podcast series is a great way to remain connected with people who are not yet ready to make an investment. It could also be a great call to action if you're unable to sell from stage, but are providing further valuable information for the audience to access. It becomes a win-win as you are building your list and now have an opportunity to continue nurturing that relationship.

c) Example: Upselling Customers – Professional Accounting Firm

Ultimate goal: To upsell services to existing clients who aren't aware of your additional services.

An Accounting Firm once expressed to me they wished they had an opportunity to share more about the valuable services they offered to existing clients. However, many of their clients only came in once a year for their annual taxation returns. "If only they knew we could offer them WAY more than just tax and compliance services," was their comment.

Here's the idea I proposed.

- They had a number of existing ways they communicated with their current clients, with their newsletter being one major way.
- Consider launching a podcast with the goal of strengthening relationships with existing clients (to avoid competitors from poaching them), however also to educate them on additional services.
  - A podcast was not an infomercial but rather strategic storytelling and speaking into the challenges they knew many of their clients were facing, showcasing existing clients who had addressed these challenges with their help, and the positive impact this had on their businesses.

- Integrate the podcast with the other methods of communication that are working well. For instance, their newsletter can be used to enable existing customers and newsletters subscribers learn about the valuable information being shared on the podcast.

d) Example: Raising Investor Capital

Ultimate goal: Startup in the technology/share economy industry looking to build brand awareness while seeking to raise investor funding.

One of my clients was a startup in the share economy and used her 5-part podcast series as part of her content collateral as she visited main capitals across Australia presenting her business to potential investors. She had created an Investor Deck along with a podcast series with the podcast series diving deeper into various details about the business to further engage with and educate potential stakeholders.

Each episode showcased a different facet of the business, targeting guests, hosts, sponsors, and investors with each building on the other. The last episode in the series tied everything together and validated why investing in her company was a sound business investment. The last information I heard about her was that she had raised over half a million dollars in funding with more conversations in the pipeline, with a projected outcome of over one million dollars.

e) Example: Building Thought Leadership (Impact, Influence and Income)

Ultimate goal: To showcase expertise, pique interest in services, and ultimately generate leads, enquiries, and high-paying customers.

Everything mentioned in this book. Especially a Thought Leader Podcast Series. (See the next chapter – Chapter 4: Tactic).

f) Example: A Co-hosted Podcast

Ultimate goal: To showcase expertise of each co-host, pique interest in their individualised services, and ultimately generate leads, enquiries and high-paying customers to each of their respective businesses.

Thinking of starting a co-hosted podcast? My first podcast was a co-hosted show, which we produced for two years. It was a steep learning process, considering many people didn't even know what a podcast was, and there were no resources to turn to. Hence, as previously mentioned we struggled to monetize our podcast.

Since that time (and another co-hosted podcast under my belt), I've learned a lot about what it takes to ensure a co-hosted podcast works for BOTH hosts. Especially if each host has their own business separate from the jointly-produced podcast.

If you're thinking about starting a co-hosted podcast be mindful that you consider these things FIRST so you can get the best results from all of your hard work:

- Your Brand Voice, unique message, and overall experience you want to create, as you bring both of your expertise, voices, styles, and mannerisms to the conversation;

- Get clear on co-hosts core values, where they're at in their business, their ideal clients, and the vision they have for their own business, before you jump in to create a co-hosted podcast.

If either of the core values are in conflict, or if one of your must-have core values is unimportant to your co-host, you may find it difficult to work together.

Also, if your ideal clients are different from your co-hosts and there are no common similarities to your audience (i.e. ideal customer), you may both struggle to generate results. Or, only one of you will generate results or better results, which can lead to the other host leaving the show.

I've had a number of conversations with individual businesses considering co-hosting a podcast. While they would have been able to create an engaging atmosphere for their listeners, it would have been difficult for both co-hosts to leverage equal results from the podcast, because each host was targeting a completely different audience. Therefore, they would have struggled to niche their show to a specific audience.

- And, most importantly, confirm your ideal client is similar and map out your Podcast Profit Pipeline to ensure a streamlined journey for your listener as you engage, educate, and entice them from your podcast to your list.

This will ensure you both receive equal share in the visibility, and ultimately leads and enquiries being generated.

> **Get into Action: Stage 2: Plan a Strategy
> for Your Unique Situation**
>
> - Decide the ultimate goal (and purpose) of your podcast
> - Map out a strategy for your unique situation

TACTIC

1) Your Thought Leader Podcast Series

I was speaking to a prospective client who was taking his decade of experience in the corporate arena and starting his own business. Even though he'd secured a few speaking opportunities, he still knew there was work to be done to build his reputation as a Thought Leader. Hence why he was considering a podcast.

Another podcast specialist recommended he waits until he had 2,000+ new contacts before launching a podcast. However, I recommended we create a 3-part podcast series to begin building his list. With the right sequence of emails, he could begin to generate enquiries, more speaking opportunities, and clients from the get-go. Because once set up correctly, your Thought Leader Podcast Series can work for you around the clock, adding new contacts to your list, who are now going to receive your nurturing email sequence as you continue to build 'know, like and trust.'

a) What is a Thought Leader Podcast Series?

A well-thought-out and produced Thought Leader Podcast Series is (typically) a 3-part podcast series that enters a conversation which your ideal client is having around the challenge they are facing; provides valuable insight into that challenge by showcasing your expertise and Thought Leadership; and compels the listener to want to know more from you and about you.

Each episode of the podcast series:

- is a standalone piece of content that strategically and subtly seeds into the other two episodes, therefore compelling listeners to access all three;
- has a clear call to action that encourages listeners to access the full series, along with transcripts and additional highly valuable resource(s).[*]
- in order to access the entire podcast series, the transcripts and other resources the listener is directed to a web page (i.e. squeeze page) where they will be required to provide their name and email (at a minimum).

Essentially, your Thought Leader Podcast Series is your Irresistible Signature Giveaway, often referred to as your free gift/lead generation opt-in. It's important to note that your Thought Leader Podcast Series is the first three episodes of your podcast with everything set up prior to your podcast launch. This means you can begin building your list with ideal clients as you continue to publish each subsequent episode, whether you're interviewing guests, or you're on your own in your subsequent podcast episodes. Your call to action at the end of your podcast episodes is for listeners to access your Thought Leader Podcast Series.

[*] Additional resources could include a checklist, scripts, quiz, further examples, etc. – something that will provide additional learning towards their desired outcome.

THOUGHT LEADER PODCAST SERIES

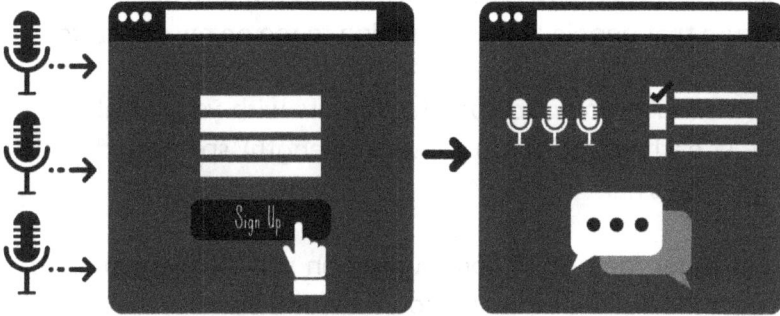

b) Benefits of a Thought Leader Podcast Series

There are many benefits, including:

- Building your list with your ideal client so you can establish a relationship as you nurture him/her with your email sequence to build a deeper level of 'know, like and trust.'

A well-thought-out email sequence can have between 7-12 (or more) touch points to deepen your relationship with your prospective ideal client. In my campaign funnels, I have eight emails as part of the podcast series. Even then, a majority of prospective customers are still not quite ready to buy, so my weekly newsletters enables me to remain top of mind, until such time they are ready.

Writing is something I enjoy, so I've had a weekly newsletter for as long as I can remember – even when I had my career consulting business. Subscribers who had been on my newsletter for months (if not years) would email me saying: "I've been receiving your newsletter for a while now, and have been enjoying learning from you. I haven't been ready to work with you previously, but now I am. Please let me know the next steps."

That continues today. Although, more frequently, due to this fact, I'm sure that people are also listening to me on my podcasts.

- You're going to spend 1.5 hours with your ideal client (if each episode is 30 minutes in length), speaking directly to him/her.

What other method of communication will enable you to speak to your ideal client for that amount of time because they WANT to access your information? We know people are busier than ever today and therefore more reluctant to sit staring at a screen. Providing them with a podcast series, which they can download and access on their mobile device, means they'll be far more likely to consume your content as they listen to your series while performing other activities, such as driving, exercising, etc.

I have colleagues that typically listen to podcasts while they are commuting to and from clients' premises, mowing the lawn, or having a bath. I'll often catch up on my favourite podcasts when I'm doing my ironing (which I don't particularly love, so listening to a podcast helps the time go much quicker, as I'm being educated and entertained) or driving.

- Audio content; build a deeper connection with people who listen to your voice.

There's something special about the bond you can create and the influence you can have with someone who has spent time listening to you. With the right sequence, powerful insights and learnings, coupled with the right stories enables you to influence a deeper level of connection with your listener than if they were reading your content in an article (or book), or watching a short video. People will often scan through written material and bring their own perceptions and understanding (and in most cases 'misunderstandings') to a conversation. Whereas, on a podcast your tone, resonance, pace, and rhythm of your voice can take your relationship to a much deeper level of trust that is often impossible to achieve through any other method of communication.

- Increased likelihood of someone requesting access to your podcast series if you are planning on sharing this as your call-to-action on your own podcast or you as a guest on someone else's podcast.

People who are listening to your podcast and other podcasts obviously enjoy listening to podcasts. Therefore, give people an opportunity to learn more from you in an audio format by giving them further information via a podcast series. Whether you're sharing this call to action from your own podcast or as a guest on other people's podcasts.

Remember, some people dislike reading; therefore, they aren't going to read an ebook (or even the first few chapters of your book). Nor do many people have time to watch long videos. So, providing content via audio format, which is in the mode of communication they're accessing and learning from the podcasts they're subscribed to, will increase the chances of your ideal client signing up for your Thought Leadership Podcast Series.

NOTE: My own Irresistible Signature Giveaway – my Podcasting with Purpose Free Mini-Training is not only audio, but video (slides) and a transcript. I've given my new subscribers a selection of ways they can consume my content, through audio, video, and written methods of communication.

As a side note, I shared this viewpoint during a podcast interview and one of the listeners agreed and shared his own experience. He learned a valuable lesson on being mindful of the mode of delivery of his content. After hearing that video is a must, he changed his written newsletters to a video newsletter. One of his subscribers emailed him to let him know that he was not going to watch a video as he was not clicking out of the newsletter, nor going to watch a video.

As a further exercise, the business owner surveyed his entire email list and the response was overwhelming. They preferred to read his content, which is why they signed up to his newsletter. They weren't interested in watching his content via video and therefore didn't watch the videos he was sharing.

A valuable lesson.

- Bypasses scepticism and objections of your ideal client

Due to the interview-style format, where I interview my clients for their Thought Leader Podcast Series, my client is able to bypass scepticism and the typical objections their ideal clients may have. This is due to my approach, the carefully structured and well thought out questions I ask, along with case studies, statistics, and other content we weave into each episode.

This would almost be impossible for my client to achieve were he/she speaking alone on the podcast, as the content would sound like a lecture and that he/she was coming across as self-promoting and arrogant.

c) Promoting your Thought Leader Podcast Series

Where can you promote and leverage your podcast series? Everywhere. I wouldn't expect you to do something I'm not doing myself (or haven't previously done myself), so let me give you some examples on how I'm leveraging my podcast series and encouraging my clients to promote their podcast series.

- Share with your existing network and/or people who have expressed an interest in your work.

Publish all three episodes of your Thought Leader Podcast Series at once, as they will be the first three episodes of your podcast, and what you will be directing people to as part of your Call to Action.

Reach out to people whom you have an existing relationship with and that you know could benefit from the information you provide. This includes contacts in your networking groups, both online and offline.

Re-connect with people who have expressed interest and enquired about your services. Your podcast series could be a valuable resource for them and a great way to re-establish a conversation.

If you have an existing mailing list that you're in regular communications with (which you should be doing as part of your relationship building), create a Podcast Series Launch email sequence and share with your newsletter subscribers, giving people a heads-up on when it is launching. Once it's been published, send out a solo email to your database, let everyone know, along with the benefits they'll gain through listening to it. Continue to share your podcast series with people you have met at networking functions who have expressed interest in learning more about the work you do.

Often, my conversations with people at networking functions spark their interest in wanting to learn more about what I do. Then, I suggest I give them access to my podcast series, which goes much deeper into answering their questions. Now, with their permission, when I send my follow-up email (or connection request via LinkedIn) I'll also send them a link to my podcast series, as promised.

- Add a link to your podcast series on your online bio across every social media platform.

Example from my Twitter Handle @AnnemarieCoach:

The Podcasting Queen | From Invisible to Influential with a Done-For-You Podcast Series for #ChangeMakers. Find out more here: www.PodcastingWithPurpose.com/PodcastSeries

- Refer to it in your bio at the end of articles you're sharing on your own website.

Struggling to get clear on your Thought Leadership message so you can cut through the clutter and become an influential voice in your industry with your own podcast? Access our Free Podcast Mini-training at: www.PodcastingWithPurpose.com/PodcastSeries or book in to speak with Annemarie here: www.PodcastingWithPurpose.com/Contact

- Refer to it in your bio at the end of articles you're sharing on other people's platforms and/or on social media platforms (such as LinkedIn).

I wrote an article for a colleague's website:

Thought Leaders: Are you leveraging podcasts to build influence, engagement and trust with your ideal client?

Here's the bio I used.

About the Author:

Annemarie Cross - Founder of Podcasting with Purpose Podcast Training & Production Company is an Award-winning Podcast Host and Producer – dubbed: 'The Podcasting Queen' as a recognised pioneer in podcasting by her clients and community.

She helps ambitious Change Makers and Thought Leaders go From Invisible to Influential with her Done-With-You Podcast Platform and/or Done-For You Podcast Series. You step up to the microphone to record your podcast and her team do the rest, without you ever having to worry about learning technology, audio post-production or even promotion. We do it all leaving you to focus on what you do best! www.PodcastingWithPurpose.com

- Use it as the resource when you're speaking and unable to sell from the stage.

Give information about it throughout your presentation with the call to action encouraging people to access it. Or better yet, collect cards, do a drawing for a winner for a special prize, and let everyone know that they won't miss out, and that you'll add them to your podcast series.

For example, at the end of my presentation, I say:

"I've only just scratched the surface today with some of the strategies and tactics you can implement in order to become known as an Industry Thought Leader in your industry with a podcast. For more information, along with some low cost and no cost tools to get you started, go to: www.podcastingwithpurpose.com/minitraining

- Use it as your call to action as the resource people can access when you're being interviewed on other podcasts and other media interviews, such as radio, TV, magazines etc.

At the end of your interview, say:

"I've only just scratched the surface with what I've shared today around how you can build your self-confidence as a podcast host and interviewing guests. If you want to take your learning further, as well as get 31 conversations starters to know what to say during those awkward moments when you don't know what to say, go to: www.podcastingwithpurpose.com/iwpminitraining

- Use it as your call to action for your own podcast, if you decide to have an ongoing podcast.

For instance, I've had a professional voiceover artist read the following script, which we've mixed with the intro music (to keep in line with the audio branding), with the intro saying:

"You've been listening to the Ambitious Entrepreneur Show. Do you want to become an influential voice in your industry with your own podcast? Access our free mini-training where we'll show you how to become known as an influential voice, along with our no-cost and low-cost tools to get you started. Go to:

www.podcastingwithpurpose.com/minitraining. That's www.podcastingwithpurpose.com/minitraining.

- Create and setup evergreen social media posts that alert people to it. Remember to add relevant hashtags so you can capture the attention of your ideal client who you know is following those specific hashtags.

Annemarie Cross @AnnemarieCoach · 5 Sep 2018

Think you need to publish a regular #podcast to generate leads and clients? You don't! Create a #PodcastSeries

Here's how we're using a podcast series strategy with other #ChangeMakers. That's #PodcastingWithPurpose bit.ly/2Lgd5Rt

Podcast Series

1 2 3

❝ People often assume you need an ongoing podcast to get results. You don't.

#PodcastingWithPurpose

d) Businesses that Have Used a Thought Leader Podcast Series

Not sure whether your business can leverage a podcast series?

I've worked with businesses from diverse industries who are now leveraging a podcast in order to add value to their listeners with the information they're sharing while showcasing their expertise, including:

- Business Networking Group
- Membership Groups
- Property Investment
- Relationship Coach
- PR & Media
- Technology & AI Business
- Share Economy Startup
- Finance Credit & Risk Business
- Lawyer
- Salt Lamp Retailer
- Brand & Business Consultant, to name a few.

If your business has a message to share and a unique story to tell, a podcast (and/or podcast series) is a great way to share it.

e) Repurposing Your Thought Leader Podcast Series with additional Content Development Strategies

When creating your Podcast Series if you want to touch all bases for varying communication styles of your new subscriber, consider creating a video (PowerPoint slides will suffice if you don't want to do face-to-camera) as well as a transcript of your content for those people who do want to download, read, and highlight important paragraphs that are most relevant to them.

When I'm working with clients to produce their Podcast Series we record video as well as audio, as well as having the podcast transcribed. This video and transcript content is repurposed and leveraged as part of an even bigger content development strategy, which includes:

- The various topics discussed on each podcast episode is broken down into various blog posts, which then directs people back to the original podcast episode, which then directs people to sign up for the entire podcast series.
- The video is cut into 1-2 minute video tips, which is shared across social media channels, which then directs people back to the original podcast episode, which then directs people to sign up for the entire podcast series.
- The transcripts of each episode are reviewed, with key sentences re-written as Signature Quotes, which are created into Quote Graphics. These are then shared across social media channels along with a comment that directs people back to the original podcast episode, which then directs people back to the entire podcast series.

All of these additional pieces of content are then set up on a social media scheduling platform, such as Buffer or SmarterQueue (which is the system I use).

PROMOTING YOUR
THOUGHT LEADER PODCAST SERIES

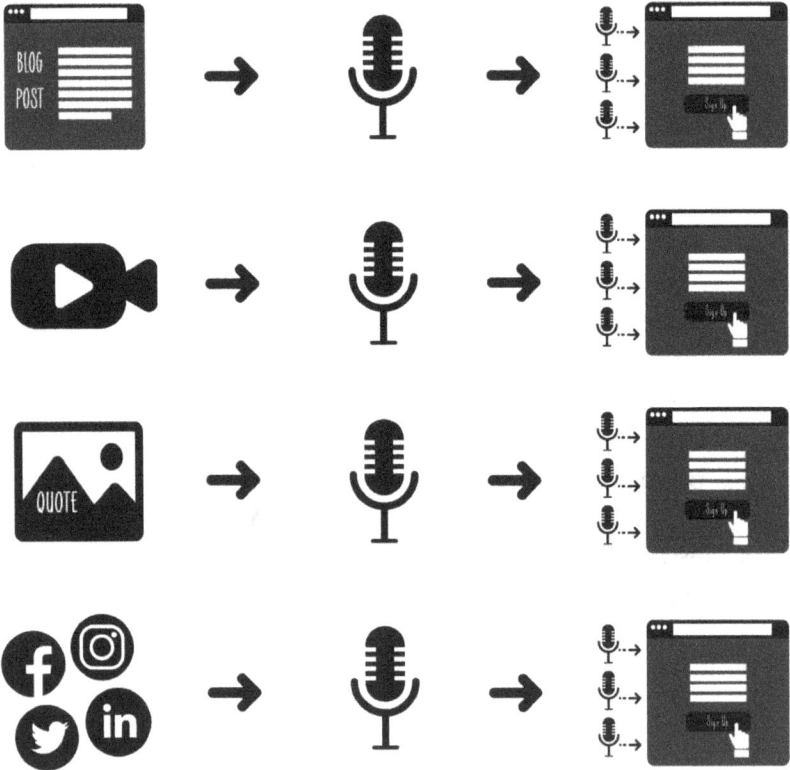

Get into Action: Tactic

- Plan out your 3-Part Thought Leader Podcast Series including:
  - Series Title (if applicable)
  - Topic for each podcast episode
  - Content for each episode
  - Additional resources for the podcast series
  - Call to action at the end of episode
- Record and produce your Thought Leader Podcast Series

CHAPTER 5

U [YOU!]

In a highly competitive industry, while you may be talking about similar topics as many other podcast hosts, the ONE thing NO-ONE can copy is Y.O.U.

A mentor once said to me: "They come for the content. They come back for the host. They come back to listen to your podcast, because of YOU!" Because, while you may have different guests on your podcast, or you bring different viewpoints to the discussions in your industry - the ONLY thing that's a constant in your podcast is YOU!

So:

- STOP focusing on what your competitors are doing.
- STOP worrying that your experience and/or knowledge is not enough.
- STOP waiting until you're ready and for everything to be perfect.

Instead, get totally clear on your distinguishing features and that unique approach that only you can bring to the conversation. Because it's those qualities and characteristics, coupled with your message that'll enable you to create a unique experience that only you can bring. Along with the unique promise of value that only you can offer - that your ideal client will love.

Then do more of that. With intention. With purpose! Because that's what'll truly set you apart.

1) The Distinction Triad

The Distinction Triad is something I developed after observing one of my former Executive clients. I'd been working with her over several years in my career consultancy; however, she reached out a few years following the closure of my career practice.

I wrote about my discussion with her Facebook post, because it moved me. Seems many of my friends felt the same way from the dozens of comments and messages I received after they read my post. Hence, I'm including my original post as it speaks beautifully into what I want to share with you in this section.

I've been doing some reflection in the wee hours of this morning.

Early this year, I shut down my Career Practice. (For those of you who have only just connected with me, over the last few decades I've worked with professionals/executives, writing their personal marketing documentation, and honing their interviewing skills.) I've spent thousands of hours coaching people in interviewing. It was so rewarding to help people gain the confidence that enabled them to see the value they offered a new employer while negotiating tens of thousands (if not more) in their salaries.

While I enjoyed the work, especially when people would let me know they 'got the job!!!!!' - I just didn't have the same level of passion for it like I once did. It just wasn't challenging me anymore. Plus working on developing a resume - especially at senior level, can take days. Days! Especially if you need to wade through pages of information and achievements and overcome challenges, and then solidify that into a few pages of WOW-ness, that has the recruiter/key decision maker saying: "We need to get this person in RIGHT now!!!'

Anyway, last week one of my former clients rang. She'd moved to another state and had decided to work with another career consultant. However, she felt that person just didn't get her. I explained I wasn't offering those services anymore. However, I heard the disappointment in her voice, as she explained what she had been able to accomplish and that she had finally, after all these years, found what she was passionate about. That was to lead to strategic leadership and transformational change projects to impact the people, the organisation, and their customers. It was then I realised I was speaking to a Change Maker, an Influencer who through her expertise was making a difference. So, I agreed to help her.

[Well, to be honest, I think it may have been her comment: "Annemarie, every one of your documents got me an interview, and I now feel totally confident about the person you had written about in these documents all those years ago. I finally recognise my worth and what I can offer."]

Yep. That got me. And can I say that yes, it has taken me hours and hours to work on her documentation, with another few hours today on the selection criteria. But it's been so worthwhile. Because here is a woman who started off as an Office Manager, who through hard work, commitment, ongoing professional development is now championing change and transformation within semi government organisations who are responsible for multibillion dollar infrastructure projects. And she is leading with her head AND her heart. She exudes everything leadership experts claim is needed to be a good leader. She leads with a strong vision and a results-driven attitude AND this is blended and balanced with an empathetic, people-focused approach. Your Attitude AND Approach - are key.

So, morale of the story - NEVER EVER limit yourself by thinking it's not possible, you are not good enough, or (fill in the gap). My friend, focus and leverage your talent and strengths and remain committed to excellence in what you are doing now, continue developing those areas you need to strengthen and grow in, and surround yourself with people who support you AND who will pull you forward. If you are the smartest person in the room - get out of that room and find one where people are ahead of you and can impart their knowledge and experience.

Just working with this client this week has given me an incredible insight into so many areas. I hope through reading this, you can gain some golden nuggets too.

Here's to harnessing your Aptitude and changing the game with the RIGHT attitude and the RIGHT approach!

THE DISTINCTION TRIAD

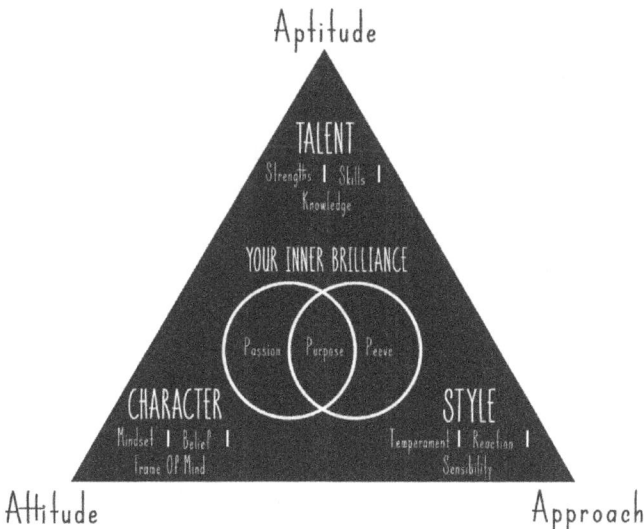

Aptitude

TALENT
Strengths I Skills I
Knowledge

YOUR INNER BRILLIANCE

Passion Purpose Peeve

CHARACTER
Mindset I Belief I
Frame Of Mind

STYLE
Temperament I Reaction I
Sensibility

Attitude   Approach

Let's begin with getting clear on your Aptitude, Attitude and Approach:

a) Your Aptitude

- What skills have you developed over the years in the various positions and work experience you've been involved in?
- What certifications/courses have you studied?
- What knowledge have you gained through hands-on learning/experience?
- If you've completed the Branding with Archetypes Assessment, looking at your Primary Archetype:
  - What strengths are listed in the description of that Archetype that perfectly describes YOU?
  - What are your gifts?

b) Your Attitude

- List 5-7 of your core values.
- Why are these important to you?
- How are you bringing these values to life in the experience you create for your clients and community as a whole?
- If you've completed the Branding with Archetypes Assessment, looking at your Primary and Secondary Archetype what are the top 3 – 5 words that describe you?

c) Your Approach

- How would you describe your temperament?
- How do you want other people to describe you? [Hopefully these match. If not, you have some work to do].
- Think about that 'thing' that fires you into action, i.e. your 'Stand for'. List 3-5 words that best describe your reaction

(in a good way) and how you want other people to describe you. [Hopefully these match. If not, you have some work to do].

- If you've completed the Branding with Archetypes Assessment, looking at your Primary, Secondary, and Lowest Scoring Archetype, list a blend of 5-7 words that captures a blend of unique style and approach you want to become known for?

Get into Action: U [YOU!] The Distinction Triad

- Define your Distinction Triad, including:
  - Aptitude
  - Attitude
  - Approach

---

2) Defining Your Thought Leadership Core Message

I believe the key to your Thought Leadership message is this. It's a blend between:

- Elements of your Personal Journey that's relevant and of value to your ideal client;
- Your expertise;
- Ways you are challenging and changing the status quo in your industry.

a) Your Personal Story

The fact that you're reading this book shows me you want to influence positive change in your industry to make a real difference in the lives of others. You believe there are rules in your industry that are meant to be broken, re-written, or completely overhauled.

I have an important message for you when it comes to your personal story.

...it's something I've come to realize is vital when it comes to standing out and sharing your message specifically for Innovators, Influencers, and Change Makers. Be mindful of the approach you adopt when crafting your story. The story where you share your personal journey - the journey that has lead you on the path to where you are today. Many of the 'typical' approaches that others teach just won't work - for you. Because you're anything but typical. You know those strengths, talents, and gifts that others often admire about you? They're not just some random things you're able to do. They were chosen, just for you. You know those heartaches, the challenges you faced, those nights you cried yourself to sleep hoping that no-one would see just how sad you were?

My friend, those moments were developing the courage, strength, and determination you now need. Because the message that's been placed on your heart is not by coincidence. It's not just some random thing you've got an interest in. It's what you stand for. It's YOUR cause. It's your Purpose; your calling. And, it's been there all along from childhood.

With every moment, every action, and every interaction - guiding, strengthening, and nurturing in you, what you need to BE the difference and MAKE a REAL difference in the lives of the people you have been called to support.

Let me give you two examples of my personal story.

My first story was when I was in the career industry. The other story about how I got into podcasting, which is a question I get asked all the time.

My Personal Story that led me into the career industry:

Note: This personal story was specifically used for my About Me page on my website as it reflected elements of what I knew my clients were currently struggling with. I'd also share relevant snippets of my story on radio and television interviews as well. I selected the appropriate points that were relevant to the topic and audience, and shared those aspects of my personal story.

"A horse riding accident at the age of 15 turned my entire world upside down. It was March of 1983 when it happened. My girth strap snapped causing me to fall off my mount with the blow to my head as I hit the ground causing a concussion. At least that was what I was told, as I still cannot remember that event from a few hours before through to the next day.

Following the accident, I began to experience frequent headaches, a loss of concentration and inability to study, preventing me from continuing my schooling. I had dreamed of being a teacher, planning to complete Form 6 and 7 at college, and then going on to university to get my degree. However, the accident changed that, because for the next six months I attended a concussion clinic at the local hospital undergoing extensive treatment to strengthen my memory and concentration.

At the completion of the treatment there were only a few months until the end of the year, so it was decided that I would return to school and repeat Form 6 the following year, while getting a part time job until that time. After a month of working in a small milk bar, my parents thought that rather than returning to school I could continue working while attending night school to further my education. I could not imagine myself working in a milk bar for the rest of my life, so it was not long after that I secured an Office Junior role with a health food company. What surprised me was that I absolutely loved it. I say 'surprised' as it was something I thought I would hate, vowing never to work in an office. The 'just in case' subjects I took at school, namely 'secretarial practice' and 'accounting', ended up providing me with the knowledge to shine in this new role, and it was not long after that I was promoted and received two subsequent pay rises. I returned to night school, completed a number of accounting subjects, and steadily worked my way up to an office management role.

Six years on, working in various office management, bookkeeping and administrative roles, marriage, and my first child, I left the 'paid' workforce to take on the role as primary carer for my family. After a year of being at home, I began to get restless so bought my first P.C. and established a secretarial business. During this time I also continued my studies (in accounting) and later within business management with an emphasis on human resources. Once I began my studies in human resources, something clicked – I had found a subject that I was totally enthralled by and wanted to learn more about. So I also enrolled in a counselling diploma, majoring in Workplace Issues and career counselling, as well as a handful of additional certificates in resume writing, interviewing, and other career related topics.

After having left the workforce and undergoing further self-assessments, exploration, professional development, and self-reinvention, I underwent another career transition to that of a Career Coach & Workplace Counsellor, and now operate my own career consultancy. It is in this role that I truly believe my passion lies, in serving and supporting others in discovering their own passion, allowing them to regain meaning and purpose in their work – something which I experience each and every day.

Upon reflection, my entire career path seems to have been prompted by serendipitous events – unexpected opportunities that have seen my life evolve from one career path to another. But then I believe that it was a higher power guiding me down that path, allowing me to discover who I was truly meant to be - serving in a role that allows me to use my gifts and talents to ultimately fulfil my life's calling. Am I sad when I think I was not able to live my dream of being a teacher? Absolutely not, because in my current role I hold training workshops; so I have been able to incorporate my love of educating and supporting people in their learning and personal development. I can honestly say that I love what I do and am thrilled and honoured to be able to support you in your discovery of your purposeful career through our *Pursuing Your Passion – Purposeful Careers* program.

I would like to share with you a passage from a book titled "Purpose Driven Life" by Rick Warren, which holds significant meaning for me. In it he writes:

> *"The way in which you define your life, determines your destiny. Your perspective therefore influences how you invest your time, use your talents, and value your relationships."*

My hope for you is that over the next 90 days we spend together, not only will you achieve significant and powerful changes in your career, but also through other areas of your life too! Here's to the discovering and living your purpose driven life and career.

Here's to living your calling!"

My Personal Story that led me into starting my first podcast:

"In 2008 I was working in the career industry and it was that year the Global Financial Crisis hit. One of my clients was a USA-based Career Organisation, where I coached professionals and senior executives with their presentation and interviewing skills.

Following the GFC, it was heartbreaking to hear about senior executives who were applying for any roles they could, with senior accountants putting themselves forward for bookkeeping and administration roles that were paying between $3.00- $8.50 an hour.

My clients were struggling and it didn't help when traditional media (radio, television, and newspapers) continued to spread the news of doom and gloom.

It was negatively impacting the psyche of my clients, and a colleague and I felt we just had to do something to spread a message of hope and possibility.

Yes, things were tough, but not impossible. There were jobs out there, however, people needed to change their approach in locating those unadvertised opportunities. And listening to the doom and gloom (that's so typical of the media), was preventing them from tapping into the hidden job market, positioning themselves to stand out in the market place, and showcasing their value within an interview.

So, a colleague and I launched Career Success Radio to be the voice of hope, inspiration, and possibility amongst the doom the gloom. We produced that podcast for two years and impacted people from all over the globe as well as establishing solid relationships with other Career experts who we invited to join us on the show.

And, the rest is history…"

The story about how my co-host and I got into podcasting is one I share frequently, as I'm often being asked how I got into podcasting.

My co-host and I were pioneers when it came to starting a podcast in the career industry, as not many career coaches were podcasting at that time. In fact, many people didn't even know what a podcast was and I'd have to explain what it was and how people could listen to the show.

Once you've gotten clear on your story and the key elements you want to share, you can tweak it to suit different audiences and platforms.

Here's an example of a post I've wrote and shared for Change Makers in my BEtheDifferentMovement.com's group:

"As a Change Maker, there was a moment in time or perhaps even a sequence of moments that ignited a fire in the pit of your belly. Can you remember what it was? For me, I remember it clearly. Because it still fires me up when I see, hear, or sense it happening. It's negativity, lies, and innuendos that serves only to keep people stuck by creating fear, doubt, and confusion. The ONLY payoff (and benefit) goes to the deliverer of the negativity, lies, and innuendos.

My moment was the negativity (doom and gloom) the media portrayed in 2008 following the Global Financial Crisis. That spark in the pit of my belly was ignited. I knew I had to do something. And that something was to be the voice of hope and inspiration. So people wouldn't remain stuck in fear, doubt, and confusion because of the daily deluge of job losses, and the blame and shame games being portrayed. Because I realised that while things were tough - they weren't hopeless. People just needed to change their approach. And without the right attitude, I knew there was no way people could ever change their approach. Unless there was a sliver of hope that maybe, just maybe, it WAS possible for them. Which was why I began Career Success Radio. To share a message of hope and inspiration along with key steps and strategies job seekers needed to take to bounce back. And that's exactly what we did.

That was my mission. That was my purpose. That was the direction that guided us each and every day. To be that voice of hope and inspiration. It was clarity and focus which guided our efforts. It was knowing we were going to make a REAL difference that gave us the courage we needed. Because to be that voice that goes against what other people are saying can be scary. Because speaking out can also spark criticism and judgement.

My friend, as a Change Maker - you haven't been called to play it safe. To play small. To just whisper. So, get totally clear on your purpose, your mission, and your calling. And use that as a force to pull you forward. To bolster your efforts and give you the courage you need to speak out. Even in the face of adversity. So you can BE the positive change that will empower others to realise it's possible - even for them."

Over to you – what's your Personal Story and journey that led you down the path to where you are today?

- Did something happen to you personally that prompted you to follow a specific path, similar to what happened to me in the career industry?

- Was something happening that you couldn't stand by and watch. Such as the situation with traditional media spreading their doom and gloom that prompted my co-host and I to start our podcast so we could be the light of hope and inspiration amongst the doom and gloom?
- Are aspects of your personal journey similar to what your ideal client is struggling with now, so they'll immediately resonate with you as you share your story?
- Does your story evoke hope and possibility in your ideal client, because it's relevant to what he/she is struggling with and wants to overcome and are intrigued to find out more from you?

b) Challenging the Status Quo in Your Industry

Want to cut through the noise and clutter to stand out and be heard by your ideal client? Become a disruptive voice in your industry.

Here are three ways to challenge the status quo:

- Experience:

Create a new and unique experience for prospective customers to 'experience' your product/service. For example, one dog food company built a huge billboard that dispensed a sample of dog food when patrons pushed a button.

In my business, I've created a podcast about the benefits of podcasting which I share with CEOs. They get to experience first-hand what it's like to listen to a podcast while learning how they can overcome their current marketing challenges and/or how they can become an influential voice in their industry.

- Unique Angle:

Are you doing something different that no-one else in your industry is doing, with your clients getting better results, much quicker than standard industry outcomes? For example: I'm a Brand & Communications Strategist and am now leveraging my decade plus of experience in podcasting to help clients create their own podcast platform to cut through the noise and build deeper engagement with their audience - which is relatively new in the market for the clients I work with.

Previously in the career industry, I was offering coaching services via phone, email, and other online technologies while many of my colleagues believed that face-to-face was the only way for career professionals to work with clients. How wrong they were.

As social media platforms were launched, it took years for many of my peers to even consider leveraging them. In fact, so many businesses believed these platforms were just a fad and ignored them. They're still trying to catch up.

- YOU:

Your unique style and characteristics bring a fresh approach to your industry. For example: An Accountant who has a fun and adventurous outlook to life and is able to explain technical jargon (that is often mumbo-jumbo to their clients) in a practical and easy-to-understand way.

Over to you, how can YOU be a disruptive voice in your industry?

- Can you create a new and unique experience for prospective customers to 'experience' your product/service?

- Are you able to bring a unique angle to how you do business or the solution you offer that no-one else in your industry is offering?
- What unique experience, characteristics, strengths, etc. can be blended to create that unique distinguishable experience that only you can bring?

Get into Action: U [YOU!] Your Thought Leader Core Message

- Create your Thought Leadership Core Message, including:
    - Your Personal Story
    - How you will challenge the status quo in your industry

CHAPTER 6

INFLUENCE, IMPACT, INCOME

1) Bringing it all together

Congratulations for working through the last five chapters. Every step you've completed in the last five chapters will ensure that when you launch your podcast, you can begin to make an impact from your very first show.

Consistency is vital, especially when it comes to:

- Your Thought Leadership Message;
- Frequency in your publication. If you launch your show to be bi-monthly, then ensure you publish a show every two weeks and not randomly when you feel like it;
- The value you continue to bring to each episode.

Doing so will ensure you'll soon become known as an influential voice in your industry – that Industry Thought Leader.

2) The Buyer's Journey

Let's recap the Podcast Profit Formula: $S + T + U = I^3$.

We've spent time reviewing the S (Strategy) + T (Tactic) + U (Y.O.U!) portion of the formula in the last five chapters. Now, let's look at I^3, which is Influence, Impact and Income through the lens of the buyer's journey.

I like to break down the buyer's journey into three stages: (1) Awareness (2) Consideration (3) Decision.

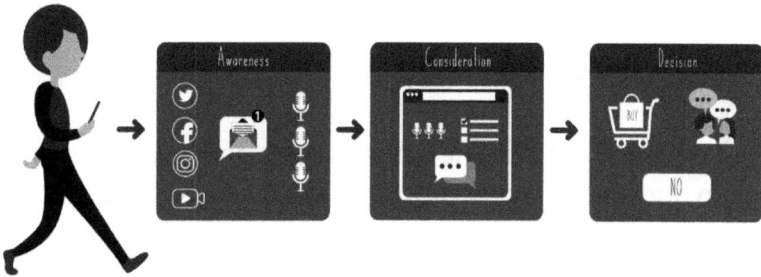

Let's have a look at each of these stages more closely and how you can leverage your Thought Leader Podcast, and your Thought Leader Podcast Series. As well as any other online/offline marketing to help nurture your ideal client along their buyer's journey so that you are the person they select to do business with when they're ready to make their decision.

a) Awareness Stage

The awareness stage is when your ideal client is aware they have an issue and are actively seeking a solution for their problem. They have found you to be a potential coach/consultant that could support them.

b) Consideration Stage

The consideration stage is when your ideal client does further research in order to learn more about the solution you offer to establish whether or not you're a good fit for him/her.

c) Decision Stage

The decision stage is when your ideal client either (a) books a time to speak with you and/or (b) purchases your product online. Or, they decide not to invest with you.

3) Your Podcast Profit Pipeline

Your Podcast Profit Pipeline is the process and subsequent tools used to nurture your ideal client through the buyer's journey.

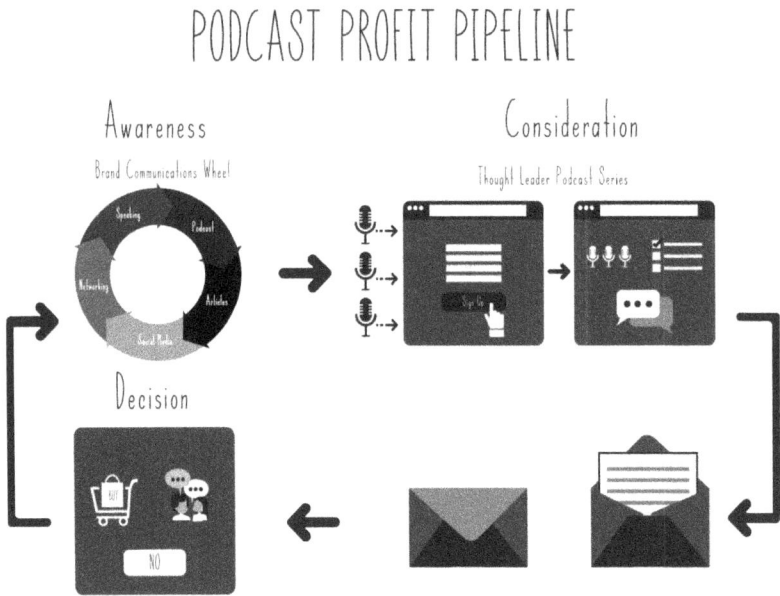

PODCAST PROFIT PIPELINE

The tools used to nurture your ideal client throughout their buyer's journey can include:

a) Awareness Stage: Your Brand Communications Wheel

b) Consideration Stage: Your Thought Leader Podcast Series
   i. Your Follow-Up Email Nurturing Sequence

c) Decision Stage: Your Call to Action, which could include:
   i.   Telephone Conversation – Let's Chat!
   ii. Product Purchase
   iii. Ongoing Communication (Touch Points) for People Not Yet Ready to Invest

Let's look at each of these tools:

a) **Awareness: Brand Communications Wheel**

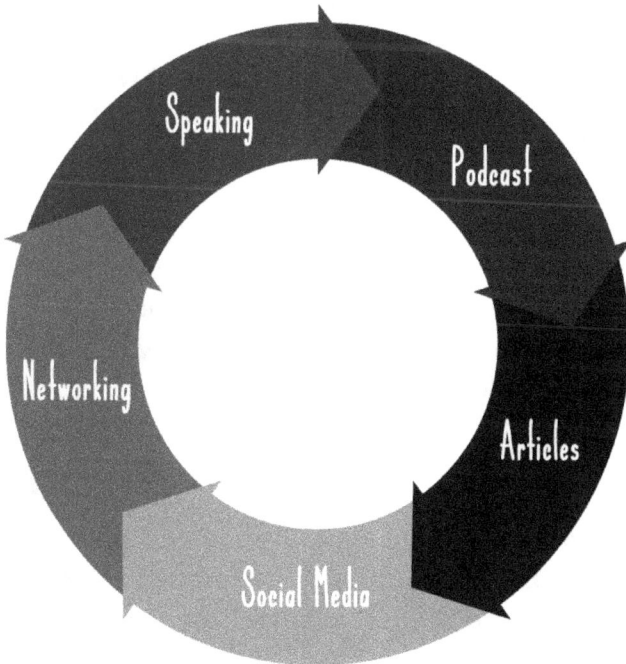

BRAND COMMUNICATIONS WHEEL

Speaking

Podcast

Networking

Articles

Social Media

Your Brand Communications Wheel identifies the various methods you will use to market your business in order to build awareness of your Thought Leadership and the solutions you offer.

For instance, you may decide your Brand Communications Wheel will include:

- Your Thought Leader Podcast
- Selected Networking Events
- Articles on your website
- Speaking (virtually and in person)
- Social Media Platforms:
    - LinkedIn
    - Facebook Page
    - Instagram

By sharing valuable content across each of these methods, you'll begin to engage and educate your ideal client with a compelling 'call to action' to entice them to access your Thought Leader Podcast Series.

b) Consideration: Your Thought Leader Podcast Series

Following your compelling 'call to action', your ideal client has now provided you with their contact details as they request access to your Thought Leader Podcast Series.

i) Follow-Up Email Nurturing Sequence:

Now you can begin to build 'know, like and trust' while positioning your Thought Leadership through the content you share, which includes the 3-part Podcast Series and additional resources you have created.

An example of a follow-up email nurturing sequence can include:

- Email 1: Welcome email [sent immediately]

  Welcome email that explains why the content in the podcast series is a must-listen and a brief overview of what he/she is going to learn.

  Also, confirm that you're here to help, so you'll send them further resources to support them.

  Include a link to where he/she can access and listen/download the podcast series and additional resources.

- Email 2: Have you had a chance to listen yet? [2 days after]

  Follow-up email to check in and see whether they've had a chance to access the podcast series.

  Let them know that you understand life and business can get in the way, so you've highlighted a few of the things they need to know immediately to support them. Include the highlights, and a link to where they can listen/download the podcast series and additional information.

- Email 3: Are we connected on social yet?

  Studies have shown that a large percentage of podcast listeners also follow brands' social media accounts, so send an invitation for them to connect with you on social media. Specifically the platforms you are most active on. (Avoid sending them to a social platform if you're not really engaging there on a regular basis).

There may even be a previous post that's generated interest and that you know will be valuable for him/her, so include that link too. Or, you may have created a Facebook Group that you invite him/her to join.

Subsequent emails in your nurturing sequence can draw their attention to a specific issue you know they're struggling with and that you spoke about in your podcast series through a case study from one of your clients. Share this information briefly within the email and then add a link to where he/she can access the podcast episode (and transcript) if he/she wants to download and read.

Remember, your email sequence is nurturing them through the buyer's journey, building your credibility as a valuable expert in your field, while also building 'know, like and trust.' You want to help them come to a decision that (a) they would like to work with you and/or buy your product, and (b) or, not.

c) Decision: Call To Action

The 'calls to action' that have worked well for me include:

i) Let's Chat:

This is an invitation to see where they're at, their goals, and how I might be able to support them. Following this brief chat, if that person seems like a good fit and my ideal client, I'll invite them into a Needs Discovery Session where we'll dive much deeper into their current situation. From there I can best recommend a solution that will support them in achieving their outcome.

ii) Purchase Product:

In my email sequence, I'll invite them to check out my Self-Paced Online Training programs in case that's a better option for them. Some people don't necessarily want to work with me on a VIP basis and are happy to go through a self-paced home study program. Plus, for my Podcasting with Purpose DWY and DFY programs, I screen people first to ensure we've a good fit and that our core values align. That's because our Podcast Network stands behind all of our clients and the message they share s needs to align with our values and what we stand for.

iii) Free Masterclass Webinar

Another step I'm incorporating into the nurturing sequence for people who have not yet purchased my product or scheduled a call with me is to invite them to a 60-90-minute free Masterclass training.

This is something I'm currently implementing in my own sequence. Those people who put up their hand will be added to another nurturing sequence, which gives them access to the Masterclass as well as follow-up emails that encourages (a) purchase of the product or (b) an invitation to chat.

For those people who do nothing, they'll roll over into the next phase in the nurturing sequence, which is my weekly newsletter.

iv) Ongoing Communication (Touch Points) for Those People Not Yet Ready to Purchase.

For people who are not yet ready to purchase, I'll keep in contact with them through my newsletter. As mentioned, some of my previous clients were on my mailing list for 18 months before they decided to reach out to have a discussion and hence make a purchase. So, sending a regular newsletter will help me remain top of mind alongside my ongoing podcasts and other content I share regularly across my social media platforms.

Get into Action: Influence, Impact, Income

- Map out your Brand Communications Wheel
- Map out your Podcast Profit Pipeline
- Write nurturing sequence of follow-up emails

PART 4

WINNING MINDSET OF A THOUGHT LEADER

Recently, at a Women's Business Conference I was speaking about how these women could share their message and elevate their Thought Leadership with a podcast. Out of curiosity, after my introduction, I asked attendees to raise their hands if they had felt somewhat uncomfortable when I mentioned the phrase: 'Thought Leader.'

The majority of women in the room put up their hand, which saddened me. Because most of the women who were in the audience were also part of the speakers' line-up and had been selected due to their expertise and the value they offered. Yet, sadly none of them recognised this. Nor did they consider they could ever be seen as an Industry Thought Leader.

What about you? Do you also have doubts about whether or not you have what it takes to become known as a Thought Leader? Does your inner critic also whisper: "Who do you think you ARE?" when you consider taking your message to a much bigger audience?

While this book is not going to add to the debate on what a Thought Leader is, or is not, I will share something that I shared with the women at this conference.

If I was to spend an hour with you and reviewed everything you had learned through hands-on experience, the knowledge you've gained through studies and certifications and through life's experiences, along with everything else that makes you – YOU, you'd be shocked to see just how much you have to offer others who are struggling and who need the knowledge, experience AND solutions you offer.

Let's look at three unhelpful mindsets that will keep you stuck if you let them.

CHAPTER 1

ADDRESSING UNHELPFUL MINDSETS

1) Imposter Syndrome

An 'off air' response from a podcast guest saddened me. We were wrapping up the show and casually chatting about her business and how far she'd come. However upon reflection and in response to my question: "Looking back over the last decade in your business, what's been your greatest lesson?"

Her response: "That until recently, I've been playing small and could have been much further along in the growth of my business. I guess that inner critic – telling me 'who was I to think I could make an impact. There were people with more qualifications, more experience, more [yada yada yada]' kept me stuck for so long."

I knew exactly what she was talking about. I've experienced Imposter Syndrome, too. And so have many of the women I've had the pleasure of working with over the years. In fact, I'd say it is one of the main reasons many women never quite reach their dreams of building a successful business that affords them the freedom they desire nor make the impact in the world, they feel called to make.

But here's the thing… and a message for YOU, if you too can relate…

As a Change Maker and aspiring Thought Leader - listening to your inner critic tell you:

- 'Who do you think you are?"

- 'You can't',
- 'You won't', or
- Any other BS.

It's NOT serving you. Nor is it serving the people you have been called to support. So, the next time your inner critic even DARES to open her mouth, before she can get a word out, tell her:

- "You CAN!"
- "You WILL!"
- Because it's what your knowledge, experience, qualifications, and every challenge and circumstance you have lived through has prepared you for, and what your ideal client needs to learn from you.

And, let her know that she's no longer welcome here. She needs to go. So, you can go DO!

2) Comparison Syndrome

Ever looked at what other people in your industry are doing and begin to feel pangs of insecurity? You begin to doubt if your knowledge and experience are enough? And how can you possibly compete with what everyone else is doing?

We ALL have. At one time or another.

Which is the reason why it's a topic that's frequently discussed on my podcasts.

But here's the thing.

It's total BS.

Because we DON'T need to measure ourselves against what anyone else is doing.

What we SHOULD be doing is getting so clear on OUR gifts, OUR strengths, OUR talents, OUR characteristics, OUR message, OUR purpose, OUR calling, and bringing these to life.

Because THAT is going to speak directly to the clients you are here to serve and support.

When you do, there's a level of inner confidence which shines through.

That's your Inner Brilliance radiating across everything you do. And it's the reason that'll attract and engage YOUR ideal client.

So, as a passionate, driven Change Maker, never EVER be concerned with what anyone else is doing.

Instead, get clear on who YOU are and the value YOU bring.

In fact, after working through the exercises in Part 3 of this book, you should now have a clear outline on your unique Signature Brand, your Thought Leader message, and valuable solutions that will continue to transform the lives of your ideal clients.

Focus on THAT.

Because THAT is the message and promise you bring to the world.

3) Tall Poppy Syndrome

Tall Poppy Syndrome, as Wikipedia describes is:

"a social phenomenon in which people of genuine merit are resented, attacked, cut down, or criticised because their talents or achievements elevate them above or distinguish them from their peers."

Has someone criticised you about your work and the message you're sharing? Yet, you know they have absolutely no basis for their comments, because of all the other comments you're receiving (from YOUR ideal client and the community you are here to serve) which are positive and thankful. Or perhaps someone has spoken over you, and because of what was said, you've now dulled a strength that when harnessed effectively is what would set you apart from everyone else?

It happened to one of my clients. Prior to opening her own business, her former bosses were threatened by her unique ability to seek out ways to improve the status quo. So they told her to be quiet. They disinvited her from meetings. It made her doubt herself and question how to leverage this strength without offending others.

But, here's the thing:

We should never dull our unique strength because it makes someone (who doesn't like change) feel uncomfortable. Or he/she feels threatened by our talents. Especially when it comes to the impact you're making with your message. As a Change Maker, you're here to challenge the status quo and set a NEW standard. A NEW standard that brings transformation and empowerment into the lives of your ideal client. So, never EVER let anyone keep you from sharing that unique and brilliant aspect that makes you - YOU!

My client certainly won't. What about you? Has someone been critical of you, so much so it's stopping you from stepping out and sharing your message in a much bigger way? Or, perhaps the fear of 'being' criticized is keeping you stuck?

Being criticised can be a gut wrenching experience. Especially if you've put your heart and soul into creating something that is now being negatively spoken about by people that don't even know you. It feels like a kick in the gut.

Years ago, a person in my networking circles told me that my inspirational messages, articles, and overall positive demeanour made her feel ill. While she did have a reputation for being negative and critical – her comment hurt. In fact, they even had me reconsider whether or not to continue sharing my inspirational posts.

Thankfully, I only considered this for a few minutes and decided I wasn't going to let her negative comments stop me from sharing my message.

If you've found yourself at the end of someone's critical tongue, or received feedback that shook your confidence and had you doubt yourself, rather than let them get to you, consider the following six things, which will help keep you focused on sharing your message, with confidence:

1. Get clear on what you stand for

It wasn't until I got totally clear on my core values, what I stood for, my Brand Voice, Brand Promise, and overall tone and message I wanted to portray in all of my marketing and my message that I was able to step powerfully and confidently behind everything I shared.

I can sum up my Signature Brand in just one word: Inspire.

It underpins my brand and what I stand for and I would defend this to the end of time, no matter what anyone says. Critic or supporter. Friend or foe. If what I have shared is on-brand with my core message, 'To inspire', then I have done my job. People can say what they want.

How about you? Are you so clear on your core values; what you stand for; your Brand Voice; Your Brand Promise; your tone and your message? Can you sum up your Signature Brand in just one word? And are you sharing a consistent message that is aligned with that one word that defines who you are and what you stand for?

When you do – you'll possess an unshakable level of confidence.

Now, when I think back to my colleague's comments, it doesn't concern me in the slightest. I know that my mission is to inspire hope and possibility in others, and that's what I continue to do. Her words had nothing to do with me, but were just a reflection of what she was experiencing in her own life. Who knows – perhaps she'll eventually find some inspiration in my posts. Until then, I'm going to continue to share them, because that's what I stand for.

2. Appreciate differences of opinions

You can speak to 10 different people about a specific topic and you'll receive 10 different opinions. And, that's ok.

Once I realised that, I was happy to have people add their thoughts to the debate and didn't see it as negative criticism towards me.

There have even been occasions where the discussion has been quite passionate and we have agreed to disagree.

A healthy debate and people's opinions don't have to be seen as personal criticism when they don't agree with you. Learn to appreciate different options, rather than take them as negative criticism.

3. Set the tone and boundaries

You set the tone and boundaries for what is acceptable, and what is not. While I am quite happy for people to share their thoughts and beliefs, it should be done in a positive and non-threatening manner. If the tone in which the other person is communicating is derogatory and offensive on my blog/website, it gets deleted. I won't participate in a conversation where someone else is not willing to have a healthy open debate. And if it's on my territory (i.e. blog/website), I'll remove them. Or, if it's on my social media platforms – I'll block them. That's not a conversation I want to participate in, period!

Would you let someone come into your home and speak to you, or other people who were in your home, in this manner? Of course not. Set the tone and boundaries of what is acceptable, and what is not. And stick to your boundaries.

4. Learn to Ignore the 'Negative Nellies'

Unfortunately, there are some people who are so caught up in their own stuff, that the only way to make themselves feel better is to criticise and bully others.

Here are three things I suggest you do:

1. Don't stoop to their level by retaliating or seeking revenge.
2. Realise it's NOT about you.
3. Surround yourself with positive people.

Ignore them. Move on. They're just NOT worth responding to OR worrying about.

5. Realise that not all criticism is negative

I'm the first to admit that I can take criticism to heart IF I let myself. So, I choose NOT to let myself. However, it's important to realise that not all criticism is negative.

Has someone said something that could help you take what you're doing to the next level? If you took a step back and looked at the comment as if it were coming from someone who had your best interest at heart – how could you learn and grow from their remarks?

I learned this lesson from my first podcast – Career Success Radio. We'd only been in production for a short time when my co-host and I received negative feedback about one of our shows.

The listener felt we didn't give the guest enough time to answer her questions before jumping in and adding our comments. The interview didn't go long enough with our guest, and she was extremely disappointed with the overall interview.

Initially, the listener's comments felt harsh. At that time, our guest interviewing skills was still developing, but after reading these comments, we felt deflated. However, after we picked ourselves up and shook ourselves off, we revisited the listener's comments and recognised we could use them to help us develop our interviewing skills. And we did. We also changed the format of our show. Two years later, our show was listened to in over 100 countries, had tens of thousands of downloads, and a regular listener base who appreciated our content.

Remember, sometimes criticism can be the impetus for transformation and improvement, if you're open to it.

6. Remember the people you want to serve

Lastly, remember the people you are here to serve. THEY are who truly matter. If your message is making an impact in their lives and you're receiving feedback to back this up, through testimonials, thank yous and positive comments – that's all that matters.

Don't let the 'Negative Nellies' stop you from sharing your message. Don't dim your Inner Brilliance because there are some people who envy you and the work you're doing.

Remember the people you are here to support. Keep all of the positive comments, testimonials and thank yous in a folder and the next time you see a negative comment – pull out the folder and read through ALL the positive feedback. Remind yourself of all of the great things you are doing and the appreciation so many people (your ideal clients and community you support) have shared with you.

They are who really matter. Everyone else? Not so much!

CHAPTER 2

A POWERFUL MINDSET SHIFT: WHAT TO FOCUS ON AS A THOUGHT LEADER

I read a quote once about the difference between winners and losers.

[Side note: I don't particularly like the term 'winners/losers' because WHO determines what a win/loss is anyway?]

The quote is: *"The difference between winners and losers is that ONE keeps going until they win!"*

What I do like about the quote is this phrase: "… KEEPS GOING until they WIN!" I'll often say to my clients (who are Change Makers in their field): "You're not just sharing your message because you want to build a successful business. Your business success will be a consequence of you sharing your message."

Obviously, there are key factors you'll need to ensure your success, some of which we've covered in this book, such as knowing your ideal client and what they're struggling with, the right message, and of course if what you're offering is something they'll invest in. However, as a Change Maker - no challenge, obstacle, or failure will stop you. You'll continue to refine your message and offerings until you DO get it right. Because your message is in your DNA. In fact, what you stand for has been nurtured in you since birth.

You HAVE to share this message because it's who you are called to be. So, when you experience disappointment, a challenge or an obstacle, get up, dust yourself off, and go again. You'll get there! You WILL win. However, ONLY, if you keep going until you do.

PART 5
TOOLS & TECHNOLOGY

LOW COST & NO-COST TOOLS TO GET YOU STARTED

Below is a list of low cost and no-cost tools to get you started on your journey to producing your Thought Leader Podcast. Because there are new tools and technologies being added constantly, I've also created a webpage, which I'll update from time to time.

The list below (and on the Resource Page) will by no means include every single tool that is available, but rather the tools and technologies I've either used myself or have seen being used effectively. Unless I've experienced a tool myself, I can't provide honest feedback. Nor can I comment on how a tool and/or technology can be leveraged in order to build influence, impact and income with your podcast.

My goal is for you to get your Thought Leadership content published as efficiently and effectively as possible in the right way and in the right order so that it begins working for you from your very first episode, without you becoming overwhelmed with all of the bright new shiny objects being added to the market.

Here are the tools my team and I use. Note: Login to our Private Client-Only Resource Page (link below) and you'll be able to click through the links provided:

Stage 1 & 2: Purpose and Plan

- Google Docs
- Dropbox

Stage 3: Produce

- Zoom [to record]
- Audacity [to edit, mix]
- iTunes [id3 tagging]

  Note: Previously I used Skype and Call Recorder for Skype (from Ecamm)

Stage 4: Publish

- Your Website
- Blubrry.com [Main hosting service I use]
- Soundcloud.com [Hosting service I've used for a few podcasts]
- Anchor.fm [app, which I'm planning on using for another podcast]

Stage 5: Promote

- Canva [to create images]
- Hootsuite [social media management platform to schedule posts]
- Smarter Queue [social media management platform – we currently use this]

- Headliner [turn audio into video to share across various social media platforms]

Stage 6: Profit

- Your Podcast Profit Pipeline
  - Brand Communications Wheel
  - Your Thought Leader Podcast Series
  - Follow-Up Email Nurturing Sequence
- Core Business Foundations
  - Your Lucrative Niche
  - Your Signature Brand & Thought Leader Message
  - Your Signature System
  - Your Signature Programs

Note: As my team and I continue to locate and leverage new tools that we know will be beneficial for our clients (i.e. YOU) – we'll update them in our Private Client Only Resource Page www. podcastingwithpurpose.com/bookresources

ADDITIONAL FREE RESOURCES

- **Industry Thought Leader Book: Additional Resources**
  Industry Thought Leaders Special Podcast Series – How Industry Thought Leaders have and continue to build their Thought Leadership with a podcast and book.
  Link: https://www.podcastingwithpurpose.com/bookresources

- Podcasting with Purpose Mini-training [Podcast Series]
  Link: https://www.podcastingwithpurpose.com/podcastseries

- Podcasting with Purpose Self-Audit Checklist
  Link: https://www.podcastingwithpurpose.com/selfauditchecklist/

- Interviewing with Purpose Mini-training
  Link: https://www.podcastingwithpurpose.com/iwpminitraining

HOW YOU CAN WORK WITH ANNEMARIE

- **Money, Marketing & Mindset Mastermind**
  THE Community for Change Makers and aspiring Thought Leaders.

  - Link: https://www.podcastingwithpurpose.com/mmmmastermind

- **Business and Career Training**
  Get Noticed, Hired and Paid What You're Worth for Entrepreneurs and Executives

  - Link: https://www.rockyourbiztraining.com

- **Podcasting with Purpose:**
  Solutions to help you go from Invisible to Influential (and Profitable) with a Podcast for Change Makers and aspiring Thought Leaders.

  - Do-It-Yourself Online Training
    Link: https://www.podcastingwithpurpose.com/podcastingtraining/

  - Done-With-You Thought Leadership Podcast Platform
    Link: https://www.podcastingwithpurpose.com/dwy-done-with-you-podcasting/

- Done-For-You Thought Leadership Podcast Series
  Link: https://www.podcastingwithpurpose.com/dfy-done-for-you-podcasting/

- **Interviewing With Purpose:**
  Become an Influential Podcast Host and Interviewer.

  - Do-It-Yourself Online Training
    Link: https://www.podcastingwithpurpose.com/interviewingtraining/

ABOUT ANNEMARIE CROSS

Annemarie Cross - Founder of Podcasting with Purpose Podcast Training and CEO/Founder of The Ambitious Entrepreneur Podcast Network - is an award-winning podcast host and producer.

Dubbed 'The Podcasting Queen' by her community, she is recognised as a pioneer in this space after starting her first podcast in 2008 and leveraging audio in her business since 2005.

Combining her love of technology, branding and digital media, she's been able to build a business, client base, and support team that is truly global by harnessing the power of social media and online technologies – particularly podcasting.

She now supports ambitious Change Makers and aspiring Thought Leaders to cut through the noise and go from invisible to influential and profitable with her Done-With-You Podcast Platform and/or Done-For You Podcast Series, her online training courses, and coaching programs.

Connect with Annemarie:

Website [Podcast Training]: www.PodcastingWithPurpose.com
Website [Podcast Platform]: www.
AmbitiousEntrepreneurNetwork.com
Website{Business & Career Training] www.RockYourBizTraining.com
Website [Personal Brand]: www.AnnemarieCross.com

Annemarie's Podcasts:

Ambitious Entrepreneur Show: www.
AmbitiousEntrepreneurShow.com
Women In Leadership Podcast: www.
WomenInLeadershipPodcast.com
The Christian Entrepreneurs Podcast: www.
TheChristianEntrepreneursPodcast.com

LinkedIn: www.Linkedin.com/in/AnnemarieCross
Instagram: www.Instagram.com/AnnemarieCoach
Twitter: www.Twitter.com/AnnemarieCoach
Facebook: www.Facebook.com/AnnemarieCrossBranding

www.ingramcontent.com/pod-product-compliance
Lightning Source LLC
Chambersburg PA
CBHW070403200326
41518CB00011B/2043